Waymaking by Moonlight

Waymaking by Moonlight

New and Selected Poems

Bill Yake

Empty Bowl
Anacortes, Washington

Empty Bowl, founded in 1976 as a cooperative letterpress
publisher, has produced periodicals, broadsides, literary
anthologies, collections of poetry, and books of Chinese
translations. As of 2018, our mission is to publish the work of
writers who share Empty Bowl's founding purpose,
"literature and responsibility," and its fundamental theme,
the love and preservation of human communities in wild places.

ISBN 978-1-7341873-4-2
Library of Congress Control Number: 2020944728

Empty Bowl
14172 Madrona Drive
Anacortes, WA 98223
www.emptybowl.org
emptybowl1976@gmail.com

Printed at Gray Dog Press, Spokane, WA
Cover art by Greg Darms and Bill Yake
Author photo by Jeannette Barreca
Cover and book design by Greg Darms
Typeset in Arno Pro

○

This book is dedicated to those who come *after*.

May the next generations find both the wilds and civility intact.
In any case, may they pitch in to mend and maintain both.

Table of Contents

Reverent and Irreverent Prayers

Desert and Steppe Poems

Forest, Mountain, and Water Poems

Brambles and Thorns—Ecopolitical Poems

Mortality

Preface

A book is a trail the mind walks. A trail is a tale, a sequence the eye can read.

As night falls, the way dims. Senses sharpen. Sounds brighten. We walk the edge and search for clues. In the Central American rainforest, native walkers attach glowworms to their sandals at dusk. Moths orient to moonlight.

These poems are offered in that spirit—attention paid to the world and markers placed by previous travelers: to the painted marks made by those who walked the desert before us, to the footprints cast in stone by ancient families tracking through tidal flats, and to the library codes on book spines.

As we work our way along stream corridors, wonder at the migration routes of flocks of waterfowl, and attend to places where brambles offer berries ripening from green to blue-black, we gather skills and memories.

～

Over time, poetry that incorporates science and silence, imagination and memory, spoken music and intuition has become a way of exploring, making, recording, and rhythmically ordering discoveries. These discoveries have been made in years and in places near and distant: from the 60s though 2020, from the Cascades and Rockies to the steppes and basins between these ranges, from coasts north to Haida Gwaii and Alaska to waterways south to Forks-of-Salmon and the Sea of Cortez; and eventually from North America into the distances of Papua New Guinea, Mongolia, Australia, Peru, Sicily, and Austria.

It has been a long, surprising, and intriguing trek.

～

This book is born in a difficult year—threats come at us out of the shadow and the glare. General civility, the earth's diversity, and biological stability teeter; the climate slips irrevocably towards storm, swelter, and thawing tundra. We go on.

Order is tentative—always the struggle to counter chaos. As chaos drops its disguises, I try to remember sunlight and how it energizes the long sequence of lives that have passed, again and again, through the needle's eye. Persistence and survival are our four-billion-year heritage. Clues and codes are passed generation to generation. Somehow life adapts.

May each of us endure to record and map our journeys—then to pass the findings along.

Of those who have provided inspiration and support—these, especially, have served as guides—suggesting, marking, and modeling routes and options—hinting at their implications:

William A. Yake, my father who—as chief of surveys for the city of Spokane—understood grids, intersections, and road alignments; the workings of theodolite, rod, and chain; order and constraint. And who—through devotion to family, Scouting, and memorized verse fragments—introduced values and possibilities including the rhythms and formalities of spoken language.

Scouting, which taught basic trail-craft: map-reading, the points of the compass, camping skills, first aid, photography, fact-finding and the wisdom of field guides.

Barbara Ellsworth Yake, my mother, who through devotion to books, reading, and note-taking, made the written word as useful and potent as the spoken word.

Amos Dolbier Ellsworth, maternal grandfather and MD, who died 9 months and 11 days before my birth. In published accounts, family stories, photos, and artifacts he imparted the magic of natural history, travel, and adventure.

Lewis Sabo, ranger-naturalist at Glacier National Park, who introduced me to the natural history of the northern Rockies—the trails, where they led, and what they revealed.

Edmund Broch, professor of invertebrate zoology, who provided the first opportunity for publication: a short, arcane paper co-authored for Oceanography and Limnology.

Howard McCord, professor of creative writing, whose poems, classes, and personal example of rambling and rock climbing, mapped routes to poetic inspiration and expression.

Jim Krull, inspired coworker, friend, and tavern philosopher who tested and trusted my judgement and intuition. By this, he bolstered my confidence in finding a way.

Heather Saunders, who got me writing poems again after years of back-sliding.

Greg Darms, friend, fellow poet, and wanderer in the high desert. Greg has suggested intriguing destinations, initiated campfire conversations, and skill-fully designed this book.

Matthew Yake, son, who—with his clever, engaged, and energetic family—sheds light. And, who—with curiosity, intelligence, and a humane perspec-tive—brightens our conversations.

Jeannette Barreca, wife and partner all these years. We share intertwining passions for natural phenomena, critters, trails, and travel. She is the planner and the one who reaches out, who keeps our external friendships intact.

Thanks also to all the other guides who have suggested destinations, pro-vided virtual and literal maps, pointed out creatures camouflaged in the un-derbrush and cryptic monuments, repaired and brushed-out trails, pointed the headlamp at goals and obstacles, and marked way-trails with blazes and subtle cairns. Among these: Robert Michael (Bob) Pyle who, for decades, has been a friend and source of inspiration, knowledge, and joy in the interest of the Earth's creatures. Former coworkers and fellow travelers, some now de-parted, who have enriched experiences and inspired poems: Greg Sorlie, Lar-ry Goldstein, Gale Blomstrom, Ann Blakley, Jean MacGregor, Rob Cole, Barb Carey, Nigel Blakley, Joe Joy, and Cedar Bouta. South Sound poets and mem-bers of the Olympia Poetry Network: especially Jim Bill, Cynthia Pratt, Chris Dahl, Carolyn Maddux, Bonnie Jones, and the late Jeanne Lohmann and Paul Gillie, as well as all the other sincere and talented poets of this exceptional town.

Thanks to the H. J. Andrews Experimental Forest and Playa at Summer Lake for residencies that provided place-inspiration and time to craft and refine poems. And to all other friends, poets and teachers: especially Tim McNulty, Gary Snyder, Jerry Martien, Derek Sheffield, Charles Goodrich, Nalini Nad-karni, Pattiann Rogers, Jane Hirschfield, Marvin Bell, Holly Hughes, and Kev-in Miller for their inspiration, assistance, and lessons in craft; as well as—in memory—Robert Sund, Lew Welch, and Richard Hugo; and the whole com-munity of poets we read and honor. Thank you.

Invocation

○

Waymaking by Moonlight

Tonight, the moon is weighted light
and shadow. When she arose opposite
the sun setting, she lit—as she rose—

in a single moment—basin and range,
wave summit and trough, plinth and pillar.
Lit, as well, a cacophony—an ecstasy—

of marsh birds: red-wings, willets, and soras.
Ibises. Now, the leucocyte moon and her luminate
stars sketch faint paths. She tugs at the core

of earth's stone, sea, and storm. They curve.
We work our worn way along shorelines,
crevasses cracked black across the ice, a fissure

broken bright against the stone. At night
the meek move. Being-by-being, stream nymphs
cast loose and drift. Moths climb from flat dark

toward the lantern's glow. Voles, pack rats,
and wolves in concert—all leave their prints
in the pale dust. This is the coyotes' hour,

the foxes', and the owls'. Moth wings—four
micro-second-hands—beat quick and wild
against cheek and scalp. The titanium light

of dream tempts the eye to close,
so the written word can turn to food,
to pathways and perceptions. Watch your step.

By moonlight we pick our way by feel:
thought and the labyrinth sense
of muscle, pressure, tendon, skin and joint

set against caution, the near-dread
of losing our bearings and the entwined
tracks of our felt obligations.

Wading thirty seconds in half a foot
of ground-fog can hobble
even a quick and nimble horse.

By trail and dead-reckoning we skirt
and transit cobble, shingle, fractured talus,
polished slabs of granite, boulders,

hexagonal shafts of long-cooled lava.
Roots worn to steps cross the trail
of mud, poison oak, fir cones,

loose stones, bound stones, and shelves
of stone; trails hidden beneath leaves.
By moonlight, color bleeds away

and only the phantom orchid glows.
We hum in our fatigue, heed the draw
and resistance of lethargic senses.

Through gloved intension and sly
happenstance we wind somewhere.
The moon is not fixed but her behavior

can be known. We search out solidity.
One more dawn to dusk.
One more dusk to dawn.

Tending Trail

*... the intelligence of deer trails is greater than that
of the speech of man.*
—Howard McCord

Through ravine and forest
we're led by the mutual
intentions of foxes, racoons,

deer, and the predatory cats—
along the game-trails,
traces, and foot-paths

that track the phrenology
of the land: its stony skull and frame
and the direct, then winding, way

its creatures find from stream
to browse, from cover to clearing,
from safety to necessity.

We have joined that trek
—being curious and wanderers—
and scramble through the maze

at first, then place a stone
for a step where the way is steep
and set cedar rounds down

in swales where swamp lanterns
thrive, in the bottom-lands where
paw prints speak precisely of intent.

Later, we'll return to brush out
sword ferns and the low cedar
fronds that crowd our tentative

human prowling; bring a mattock
to widen side-hill runs—to cut back
soil on the uphill slope, the sloughing

duff with its curled millipedes tucked
inside—the yellow-spotted, almond-
scented, cyanide-laced kind.

New fiddleheads and rich decay
will tumble from above. Then we
heap and smooth, widen and level,

rake and tamp the moist ground
down—retaining each substantial
root as foothold or intricate

step; leaving branch handles
intact to grasp—so when we come
this way, again, it will be only

a little less lightly
        than the beasts.

Flecks, Hints, and Intuitions

O

"Maximum information, minimum number of syllables."
—Allen Ginsberg

Five Lessons Learned Immediately on Getting Dumped from a Raft into a Wilderness River

One on one there's no fighting a river.
Adrenaline rivets the attention.
Attend to the advice of guides.
Of all physical entities, the most precious is air.
Roll upright and go feet-first into the unknown.

inside out

trees are our lungs turned inside out
& inhale our visible chilled breath.

our lungs are trees turned inside out
& inhale their clear exhalations.

Improvement—Resisting the Impulse

Consider the snag:
to replicate nature,
stand aside

26 June 2018

Woke this morning to a deer bedded down not 10′ away,
just outside the bedroom's glass doors.
Her ears, a little ragged, are never idle.

Saw-Toothed

Range on range of saw-toothed mountains.

No,

as Lew Welch said,
. . . getting it all confused again.

Rack on rack of mountain-toothed saws.

Aphorisms

History and rain: they teach us humility.

❧

What is wilder than light, magma, dark matter, and the crackle of lightning?

❧

The illusion that we have no illusions may be the most difficult of all illusions
to dispel.

❧

Science is most vital and functional when it balances respect for authority (the literature) with an active questioning of that authority (the experiment). All is honored, nothing worshipped.

～

As with flames, clouds are expressions of interacting variables: temperature, humidity, gas velocity, and light. They can, and often do, stand still while all within them is moving, swirling, progressing. This is a mystery. What is insubstantial seems substantial. We, too, are clouds and flames.

～

Poetry: salvation from the mundane.

Aging,

we grow asymmetrical—
strength in one eye
and the opposite leg,
and our lives gyre
slowly at first—
then like old nations
we pull in our arms
and spin thin strings of fire.

Minimalist Autobiography

[on a deep black background]
(ellipsis) I (ellipsis)

Island Bay

By Braille I go aft to piss
into a slack and moonless Sound.
Phosphorescence!

What the Albion lady, who was stomping on her onion tops, said:

It makes the roots grow
bigger.

Spring

Beneath the hail,
fresh rhubarb leaves
    pulse and bob.

Lost

On a trail among alders,
scratched sunglasses perch
on fresh bear dung.

Running into the sun,

a bee blurs by—
　　brushing my eyelid.

Fire Cooling

White limbs crackle.
Convection dance
stills to black.

Free white ash,
cool as bone.

Etymology of the Word Solve: To Set Loose

Back-peddling high in the fog
and perpetual hunger, a gull
gapes and drops
a clam to shatter
on stone.

Three Interactions

Geese call back
to the squeaking of handsaws,
to bells.

Avocados tempt panthers:
so panthers eat and plant them.

Yesterday on the fitness trail,
two apricot pits in coyote scat.

Bluff Above Calm Sea

a sort of dizziness overtakes the sky.

disparate winds within stalks of
fine grass quiver from the roots up.
grass, spring-loaded with a special notion
which is music, makes winds so narrow
they go with slim consequence.

barely mundane, crows fly below with news.

Beyond this copse of ash and oak
Bosco della Ficuzza—Sicily

the persistent cadence of the cuckoo
call in the same key as the subdued cacophony
of a dozen, hidden cow bells.

Working the Cemetery
Lake Forest Park, 1968

Weed, mow, and sweep.

If life were sacred
we would not eat

without permission,
without praise.

Remembering John Muir
Climbed Tall Trees in Storms
Seattle Hilton, 1990

Fog—streetlight yellow,
the color of aspirated sodium—

scuds up from Elliott Bay
like smoke from a forest burning.

Twenty-three stories up,
room lights out—February wind—
monumental towers of glass
sketched & polished in reflected light

quiver.

Cohorts

O

"The rhythms of our bodies and our voices are not, as we know, immune from the rhythms of things around us—lovers and neighbors and friends, animals, plants . . . these rhythms leak into poems."
—Robert Bringhurst from *Everywhere Being Is Dancing*

Lake Quinault
for Jeannette

Mushrooms you named were
Witch's Butter, Rosy *Gomphidius*,
Satan's Fingers, Angel Wings,
Boletus, Slippery Jack, and *Russula*.
Your boots were tan as chanterelles
with their gills going a little way
down the stem,
something like muscles
of your arm—how they tuck in tight
under the taut shoulder muscle.

Slide alder.

I was lost an hour in your present kiss—
in the flavor of mushrooms and mild earth,
in the delicious lines of jaw and ear.
Lost—too, this morning—seeing you
in a sky-blue night dress that fell simply
to the knee over faded jeans.

Leaning over the cook-stove,
kneading soap into your hair (suds white,
hair black) enunciating the morning,
rinsing out your hair, just that, with wood-
warmed water. Wringing it out,
wrapping it up in a glaze gray towel.

The river—bottomed with stars and stones—
filled and emptied the lake clearly and continually
until it is evening. A bluer light fills
the hills. Cedar foliage patches the dark
spruce slopes with yellow.
A mosquito lands on a wrist—
          I am not sure whose.

14 February 2000
for Jeannette

Two lights, one light, darkness, rain.
Wind chimes fuss and the cat
complains beyond the porch door.

Beneath comforters you curve
and nudge, warm as banked coals.
Constant. Thank you

for loving the perennial:
the empty stem, the stark rose,
even the black branch of winter—

and for knowing how every bed
and mound, bud and tuber
waits for inevitable spring.

Granddaughter One
Loretta Skye, b. 13 June 2015

Like a footprint
or laurel branch,
you are something
where a year ago

there was nothing.
Organized. A variation
on the theorem of
presence, the first trick

of the adept magician
—ahah!—making quick
the work of mitosis,
multiples out of division,

a handful and a heartbeat
from mere potential,
affection, and that other
miracle—biology.

Son Out of a Long Absence
for Matthew

You were born. The house burned down.

The sound of loons calling to mate in spring,
of water draining soaked lentils away,
and of laughter: all became ash and recollection.

I hooked my fist into the belly of each year.
Measured in a drumming, they echoed,
and were clocks in the attic. Months beat
their wings in my ears on days without birds
in winter.

Water drawn between steep walls, when
we spoke it was haltingly—staying clear of,
saying nearly the truth.

Now time is a resonance of hollow things:
violins, jack-o-lanterns, seed walls folding
into spines, and breath into the bones
of petrels.

There is nothing to learn here. Our lives
simply unfold as they burn, without error.

Barbed Wire

for my father, William Albert Yake

Fathers begin old, get older,
seem sure almost to the very end.
You retired, bought your farm,
a pond that dried up summers.
Cows ate the plums,
pushed over the outhouse,
wandered onto the porch.

Late summer, seven years ago,
we deepened the pond a little
dragging a rusty fresno
behind the cranky tractor—
scooping up snail shells, cracked silt.
Afterwards in the hard light
I turned to watch you sitting
on the plank ramp to the dock.

You were wearing swimming trunks
that were twenty years old,
and lathering your legs
with a worn bar of white soap.
The skin on your arms hung
loose and creased. Your shins and feet
were gaunt. I thought of walking
sticks cut from lilac branches.

For your birthday that September
I got you a roll of barbed wire
and drove south. This spring
after the second stroke, before the last,
it showed up in the shed—bright, intact.

Asking for It

Calling his sister, he asks for the truth.

You should change, she says, *but you won't.*

Picturing wrist-sized passages threading slopes of talus,
he knows that the arc of this conversation requires a single
correct response.

Years ago, he'd stood near the rapids under a streetlight.

A faint cry from that fast water was swept downstream.

Swirling snow melted into the slick black water.

What could he have done?

He was on foot, alone, and it was night.

Conversation Among Old Folks
Common Ground Farm, outskirts, Olympia WA, 5 September 2012

When I arrived, bringing a book on easing
bodily pains, Greg sat at the table holding
a diminutive, bedraggled bat tucked in his left
hand. With his right, he fed her. Chicken fat

on a toothpick and in the bat's enthusiasms
the fat proved better, even, than meal worms.
She was ravenous, worked her fanged mouth
wide. Reached with a wing to pull the fat-dabbed

toothpick in whenever it withdrew. Famished
for having been trapped, mistakenly, the night
before, on flypaper; then rescued and unglued—
no one knew if she'd eaten the trapped flies.

Talk wandered then: from bats to the glittering
chitin in their guano, swifts stalling over chimney
roosts, falcons clued to that, and aircraft crashing
—having lost the horizon in Antarctica. Nancy

cleaved plucked chickens, with her WHACK
severing thigh from drumstick, while Julie
examined books to size the absent swifts, and
for a long, long moment no one's body ached.

Silence

How am I to read a friend's silence? Silences are. Secrets. Blessings or weapons. Necessities—perhaps—or signs of confusion. [Treacherous silence.]

Words—careless or not—confuse. [Treacherous language.]

Listening confuses as well. [Treacherous construal.]

Silence at a distance obliterates even the look and stance; obliterates all footholds and handholds but memory. [Most treacherous memory.]

One night at the fire this friend spoke of walking on water. Years later he meshed calligraphy with figure painting and fell silent. His father was old as the oldest tree. The tide rose and fell. The fog rolled in. Candles on tiny boats drifted away. Because it was winter, no dragonflies emerged from the split backs of their earlier selves. A woman in the far room was making books with subtle motions of her hands. Darkness fell; the tide congealed. Once again a vision of walking on water arose in his thoughts; that, and the memory of children drowned by a great wave.

Reflected in murky water, he stood looking into fog and was silent. This fog was thickening. Nothing was quite as silent, then, as the bottom of the sea.

From time to time Lew Welch
for Lew W. and Greg D.

(In '62 from time to time Lew Welch would leave his hermit cabin
for a drink in Cecilville.)

Up the Salmon
roads get skinny
and a little scary.

Nibbles of road keep falling into the river.
Water glints among the shadows far below.

In '95 we drove up to the Cecilville Bar.

Joe Snipes ran it then. It had burned in '87.

A guy with half his heart drank
and blamed the spotted owl. *My next wife,*
he said, *will be normal.*
More whiskey.

Late, past midnight, driving back to camp,
the river falling
off to the left,
cliffs and dark sky rising
steeply
to the right:

a Bear loped ahead.

The soles of his feet
showed white
in the headlights.
For half a mile we crawled
behind

in compound low, till
he'd had enough
and scrambled
right straight up
into the night.

A Poem in Two Voices: Struggling to Distinguish
Butterfly Species: The Lupine Blue (Icaricia lupini)
and the Acmon Blue (Icaricia acmon)
for Jonathan Pelham who devised the key

Dorsal iridescent hue of cyanic overlay?
                  A thicket of specifics,
Extension of dorsal forewing marginal line
                  often barely distinguishable,
toward base along veins—absent, faint,
                  that we attempt to parse
or prominent? Caterpillars buckwheat
                  and interpret as each creature
or lupine feeders? Early generation or late?
                  goes on, not oblivious exactly
Lowland or high-ridge citizens?
                  but preoccupied with the avid,
melded, quick acts and judgments of survival.

29

Talk

for Nigel, Ann, Jeannette, Greg, Gale, Larry, and Cedar

We were drinking tequila.
There was a banjo in the corner of the room.

Nigel said, "Well, we"
—by that he meant Ann and himself —
"got this room once. Reserved
it at a distance in a resort city.
We got there and the rooms, they
were all done up in black velvet.

We got out of there fast. Forfeited our deposit.

But, then, the next room—
            it was filled with millipedes."

That turned the talk to rooms William
Burroughs would have shunned—6 layers
of stained avocado wall paint and an armed
night guard. And cockroaches—how at least
one'll always stand fast against the light.

Then
to a rain-forest cabin where packrats
scurry half the night
cross the cook stove, plastic-covered
mattresses, your bare chest.

To which Nigel mused, "I was
sitting once on the beach
at this Florida key watching the sun
go down, and this rat sidles over,
leans up against me
a minute or so anyway.

He's watching the sunset too, I guess."

And Ann—a legitimate biologist, I swear—
    she vouched for this.

Winter in the Interior
based on the experiences of Larry Goldstein

Salmon were walking up the creek bed
on their bellies when the wind blew

the sun out. Winter blew plovers south,
frogs underground and covered the mice

in dust—snow dry and squeaking underfoot.
Raven—the winter bird, white within black—

shrinks far distances down
to a single, audible wing beat. All winter

I awoke in the dark cabin, turning once
with arms outstretched before the fire.

Outside, in the long night, feathers were
tracing arcs in the repetitious snow.

I never told you this, but that
        was the best year of my life.

Bat Island

Taima, Sulawesi, Indonesia.
for Marcy Summers

It should have been the dry season, but it had rained all afternoon before
clearing. The flying foxes were late, the sky's fire out, the dusk thickening.

When, finally, they appeared—determined darknesses streaming northwest
against the obscure sky—she shouted and danced in the sand, arms stretched
and tilted like wings.

A stream of minutes and minutes and minutes.

Three thousand she thought, headed for the mainland. Last year there'd been
ten thousand. Then the bush-meat hunters sailed in from Manado. They
stayed days, netting thousands that died in kin clusters, squalling.

Then packed as treats they were shipped to the Christian north for the feasts
of Christmas.

What few bats remained did not remain. They emptied out the island. Left
its miniature forest to the insects, its beach to the nautilus shells and small
conchs, its waters to the villagers fishing off-shore—their outrigger canoes
painted yellow, orange, and blue.

The foxes flew off. Left dusk and dawn empty for months, empty but for the
waves and cicadas.

But now they were back. Diminished, yes. But a village of three thousand
pollen-and-nectar-feeding bats streamed for the mainland's fruiting forest.
And Marcy was dancing in the sand.

The image makers

enter the hill and long passage inward.
They bear torches soaked in beeswax
and pine resin, tallow lamps lit with the wicks
of dried whitewoods and juniper twigs.

Since waking to read their dreams as spoor,
these creators have bowed before
lichen-browsing bison; solitary cave
and brown bear; the arc-tusked mammoth;

snow-lashed musk-oxen; herds of reindeer
swimming summer rivers, grazers of beechnuts,
moss, and mushrooms; the skittish and serene,
the rut-singers, these potent and dangerous kin.

Those most skilled in shaping stone
etch images with the careful blows of burins,
the smoke of rock dust drifting up in miniature
bursts through torchlight. The painters of dream

evoke beasts from the black of bone charcoal
and manganese, the white clay; and shade
the belly-hollows with shadow and umber.
Already, the alchemists heat yellow ochre

in flames to summon the cardinal hues of blood;
grind pigments to powder, blending paints
from quartz, talc, pigment, cave water, and gypsum;
spread these on palettes of vertebrae and oyster

shell: colors worked into walls that arc high
into domed sanctuaries. Our ancestors' necklaces
are strung with the incisors of wild, fat-bellied ponies
whose bone cores drip sweet marrow. Pale yellow

stallions and mares with hides dappled in Isabella-blue
feed the lamps with clear-burning fat; give stiff thread
from their jet manes—hair plaited into cords that bind
the artists' high scaffolds. A day's work, a week's—

time suspends at the shivering boundary between flame-
light and ricocheting shadow, as if the stone writhed,
drew breath, and shook off long hibernation—bison
(like flames shuddering), falling horses, and a great black

leaping bull. Once sanctified, what music must have risen
from this hall of flint and limestone: diatonic bone flute,
oak handle rapped on resonant calcite drapery, xylophones
of bear skull and hip bone, bull-roarers, and ocarinas

of pierced conch, joined finally by the human cry
and song: voices that reverberate, rise and speak,
making essence from imagination at that empty
triple center: I, clan, and the otherwise still secret earth.

Regard

Pipestone Canyon, July 1998

Jeep tracks wind, hidden in the summer grass.
Grain heads whip against the hood—
loose seeds dancing from their shattered heads.

Considering this word *regard*, the narrowing
stone canyon walls, and the road trailing off—
I park and walk.

Mosquitoes rise in the dying light,
mist in the swales. And on my tongue,
the evening goes solemn
and blue as a single elderberry.

Then—an instant, insistent alto buzz.

Cicadas?   Be aware.

Winding
deliberate as a low-land river
from foot to road shoulder
where he does not coil, but gathers
up in tight meanders, raises
his anvil head ankle-high,
black tongue flickering—

the etiquette apparent:
I am here, be aware.

Assassin and Warblers

We're staying three nights at the Marriott Residence Inn in McAllen, Texas—
Lower Rio Grande Valley. Despite the single cockroach in the bathtub it's a
nice enough place.

At breakfast, a white guy with a stubbly beard, ironed jeans, and tan sports
coat is helping himself to granola and yogurt. I wouldn't notice but he's
with a small woman in black jeans: thin, fierce, sexy and Mexican. That, and
he doesn't seem aware that his sports coat has hung up—hitched over the
Beretta on his right hip.

When he turns, his neck twitches. I've seen that before, in lizards—a male
burst of color often follows. But we are here to find the migratory warblers
of South Padre Island: the Parula, the Cerulean, and another called the
Worm Eater.

The January Floathouses of John Day Slough
for Greg and Christi

A shaded, wet and windy country where
houses ride—pinned by pilings, bound
by spikes, bolts, turnbuckles and thick-
bored chain links. Dwellings hang
on the long tidal breath of this short river
constrained by dikes—float in fluid, tenuous
disquiet. A certain uncertainty. Flexing
walkways decked in asphaltic grit run
neighbor-to-neighbor along railed gangways
strung with solstice lights.

One day in clarity. One in thickening clouds.
A third in iconic rain. The sky rests on
slack water and windows consider the slick
green tension where bluebills dive to clam
in silt. Two merganser pairs—one set in rapt
pursuit, the second dawdling, dive. And
but for their splashy, skipping launches,
the coots rafted near the far bend mill
in considerable mute constellations.

Just beyond rippled window-glass a neighbor
runs his gillnetter out though early
morning rain. He's meditative, tugging
at a thermos as each twenty-seventh
raindrop on the river
leaps to form
a brief, bright
reflective hemisphere.

Reverent and Irreverent Prayers

○

" . . . to pray does not mean to send messages / to the gods; to pray means
to listen."
—Robert Bringhurst, *Conversation with a Toad*

Feeding Frenzy

We run east through Skincuttle Inlet, past Low Black Rock, Elswa Rock,
Bolkus Islands, Deluge Point, Inner Low Rock, and see at last, well out
into the strait, the first blows. Ten, then twenty humpbacks. Even more,
churning the surface, spouting as far north and south as we can distinguish.

Feeding, the whales of Hecate Strait
roll and roil in the chop where krill & herring crackle, spat
out of the sea in exhilarated terror—an awful hailstorm
of food churning among sleek whale fuselages that flex,
rise, and slew ecstatically to feast in mile-long bands
on the blood-ochre of rising crustacean-clouds. Lit by the flash
of herring, the humpbacks revel in a massage of frenzied food;
gulp, sigh and say their grace and gratitude with grunts,
groans and James Brown hallelujah shouts, *Yow, I feel good!*

࿇

The feast of whales continues as we depart for Rose Harbour where, once,
whales such as these were flensed, dismembered, and rendered. Near rusting
machinery, a small plaque faces the harbor:

IN MEMORY OF THE CHINESE AND JAPANESE
WHO DIED IN THE EMPLOY OF CONSOLIDATED
WHALING BETWEEN 1925 AND 1941

A Biology of Play

Los Isoletes, the Sea of Cortez

Immersed, buoyed, propelled
by the sea as if by a dream of flying;

on all sides the brine was a trampoline
and flung its ecstatic dolphins up.

A surrounding, it was teaching
pup sea-lions to flex and spin

like fletched arrows, to loll
belly-to-belly at the green

and flashing surface, their whiskers—
    quill-like and gleaming.

These adolescents arrived when I hummed
and played the snorkel—a rude trombone.

Peering, with a question in their eyes,
they blew bubbles at me,

and spiraled down, disappearing
with the noon light, to turn

and come rocketing back: *a cappella*

jazz dancers in aquamarine ether.

Shout of the body, song of the fin.

Winter Solstice
Nisqually Wildlife Refuge

Somewhere in the closing fog—
I hear the purposeful whistle

of wings, ducks, and the hidden
arc of their muted chat and gabble.

Without horizon, gulls perch
and blur near flat water, where

starting at my feet, I read
the cuneiform of flooded stubble.

It spells cold and calm
in water-doubled rows.

From the duff, *amanita* embers
bulge and glow. Crabapples still

hang in the black reticulated branches
of winter trees—nearly burning.

All these spare embellishments on
the ritual contraction of winter light.

The Tree as Verb

The true formula for thought is: The cherry tree is all that it does.
—Ernest Fenollosa

Seed, swell, press and push, sprout, bud, curl, bloom, unfurl, quicken, ripen, and dispense.

Remain.

Blotch, ferment, rot, and mushroom.

Germinate.

Probe, grope, root, draw in, draw up, dole out, absorb, allot, assimilate, respire, reconstitute, release.

Senesce.

Reach, brace, resist, avoid, deflect, split, notch, rustle, shake, bend, and shimmy.

Occupy.

Cover, mask, obscure, protect, enclose, and hide; tolerate, support, feed, shade, harbor, and disguise.

Stand, sketch out, stretch out, fork, reach, branch, divide, incline, and sway.

Reclaim, endure, and burn.

Return, leaf out, green up, synthesize, digest, night-quiver, yellow, wilt and wither, abscise, and collapse to root and rise.

Sketch from the Transitive Valley

... scientific thought consists in following as closely as may be the actual and entangled lines of force as they pulse through things.
—Ernest Fenollosa

I notice man sees horse grazes grass grows itself.

Wind blows seeding grass sends hay scent wafts with air through valley.

Valley funnels day breeze upstream points east breathes hay-scent air lifts moisture.

Chill makes droplet holds pollen seeds droplet grows chill.

Drop pulls earth pulls drop drops itself.

Drops join one another wet soil grows grass blooms itself.

Seeds seed grass greens valley holds me/man/horse/soil grass swells all.

All swallows one drinks pollen discolors eyelid blinks itself.

Myth, Wind, Stone, Seed
a song for fractals, myth, chaos

slow writhing magma floats and folds
this crust of wandering, stonecast plates
—and extrudes, stretches, folds and refolds
confections convected, remelted, reborn.
tilting and stretching, singing and sung,
enfolded, intruded, outcropped, and eroded—
breccia buried
   in a lengthening night of crackling ice
piled for winters and years of cool summers,
ice stretched and flowing, broken and folding:
quick rock, slow wind—rising and cooling,
falling and warming, risen and cooled
   again and again. the wind that churns,
loops, convects and billows precipitous
clouds involving full hail, back into rings,
back into stones. steep clouds (porous as air—
stretched by the eddy and yaw of the variable winds)
are streaked, banded, stretched and torn.
while over dry lakes, high ridges, far ranges,
cumulous grown in the gut of the sky—
seeding and sowing a hard random rain,
breeding and breaking branches of lightening,
their syllables Thunder!

all of the earth is rivers beginning,
branches from branches, and branchlets from these.
picking up silt, setting it down,
sorting, sifting, winding, rewinding,
bending the banks, braiding the channels.
then setting down varves—
both in low lakes and abysmal rifts
below the relentless and unquiet sea.

the exuberant grasses express and divide
seed into seed, pollen and germ—chaos
of stalks arched and blown
by ceaselessly folding, encyclical winds.
chromosomes encoding a mitochondrial contra;
dance done for nearly so long—
always just similar, never the same.
spirals of conches, cones of the pine:
winged, burred, and naked seeds.
out of the longest insistence of all—
persistent, old absolute physical memory.
 fire cones of lodgepole grown from fire;
 squirrel cones grown from squirrel.
wind and mice and seed-eating birds,
growing, dividing, grown and dying,
burning it up and growing it back.
and always this kind of memory
for the wind bringing fire
and the wind bringing rivers.
the rhythms we learn from the heart of the world,
the drum of the grouse, the heart, the footfall.
the rattle of dying, the clacking of bones,
chant and tattoo of wind bringing windstorms.
stories long repeated though never
exactly, precisely the same—hammering out
with blow after blow coastlines, fault lines,
the talus, and sand.

a coastline is broken from long imbrication,
the continuous throb of a long-ringing bell.
eelgrass drifted and woven in storm-rows,
windheap and waveheap and wind-driven spray.
kelp and the seagrasses wrapped and wound
into the surge and the roll of the sea:
middens left by the hunters, the sorters, the sea.
baskets of sweetgrass and spruce root—
each skip-stitched—embroidered with pliable stalks:

special lids topped with knobs holding pebbles
that rattle whenever the basket is moved,
   like berries.
small baskets for children, work baskets for women,
black bracken in patterns entwined and named:
   "the tattooing on the back of an old person's hand"
   "the heads of salmon berries cut in half"
   "the long line of drift along the shore"
patterns apparent from life at the center,
attentive to each ceremonial motion,
the rain-fashioned hat—
conical, two- and three- strand twined,
spruce root, skip stitch, Raven design—
worn in the winter of long-beaked masks
pointing up to the season of intricate dances,
masks wincing and shrugging
in the unsteady light of late fires—
here's where the oldest stories are told.

time stretches out—seconds thin and long,
years (with the knots of the seasonal moons)
spun and wound round songs deriving
from the mnemonic beat of the world going on.
small spring frogs throbbing like the courting
of grouse pairs—the enunciated drumming
precise and extended as if winter wrens sang
in vibrant tenor. breakers, white water
—large and majestic—arc against shadows
like slow solar flares: laminar, then turbulent,
currents of water. storm fronts blossom
at the edges of tropical and temperate seas,
the mountains are turning and constantly walking.
conversely, in the moment that one detonates,
or in the trip-hammer systole
of a bumblebee's heart,
all imaginable patterns and moments derive
and are blasted from mineral to smoke,

become impulse,
make every transition—fire, water and air—
tell seminal versions of each of these stories,
sing faultless translations of all these songs,
dance into and out of impermanent view.

Confluence

Yesterday (1, December) smoke slipped
to the ground under a long rain.
Grey into grey like young rivers
washing into an old sea.

So, I put on the hat with the owl feather,
took down the hatchet,
caught the rooster.
    There was a pause, blood on the block,
    a palsied shuddering
    dance. Blood, rain, steel, cedar.

Plucked & cleaned the rooster,
blacked the cookstove,
called my sister & finally
    considered estuaries:
    roiling dignity,
    gradients mobile
    as the topography of winter surf.

Now things must stand for themselves;
apparent & whole as a piccolo jig.

There are riddles enough—
    loops nested, one within another:
    each seductive
And answers enough—
    sworn testimony: evidence
    obvious, inductive, & inadequate.

Take, for instance, the hat feather:
    you say it is spirit,
    then gild its silver image.
I say it belonged to a scabland owl:

abetting silent claim
to the souls of mice.
Perhaps we agree.

Or the rooster,
cocksure to the end,
abiding by the poultry Tao. Dancing even
after the hatchet fell.

Which brings us at last to estuaries.
The moon makes them flow both ways,
stirs rivers into the milk-emerald sea.

The challenge is to adapt to this transitory brackishness:
to dance like logrollers—
mix blood into water,
myth into text,
equations into designs full of dreams and grey smoke.

Two Dreams

1. "As dogs, cats, horses, and probably all higher animals, even birds have vivid dreams . . . we must admit that they possess some power of imagination," wrote Charles Darwin.

Last night I dreamt of elephants of various sizes climbing playfully into an armored car in the process of making a cash pick-up. The personnel, in bullet-proof garb, were understandably nonplussed.

2. A long chart of all the notes the Grateful Dead ever played—a lower band of dots, and a higher band. To the far right and climbing, a smattering that they called "The Rising." From the stage they joke about re-entry and skipping off the upper edge of the atmosphere to be, forever, lost in space.

what buds from the ground of being, from the root of life
  soyo—meaning "sprout" in Mongolian

schools of fish & family.
the flight of cranes. each of us around this table. judges.
young hemlocks. professors & developers. newsmen & pine beetles.
granite boulders with open mouths.
speech & song, wave lap, branch & leaf.
flower & pistil. the domino. the inside straight.

To Fungi & Their Hosts—the Intimates

O you, the living & damp—
    the fungi desire to lie with you.
O you, the expired & seeking exit—
    the fungi reach out
    to break you down.
O you ancient blue-greens—
    the fungi wish to meld with you
    flesh to flesh & flourish.
O honey & barley—
    the fungi yearn to promote
    your Dionysian transformation.
O finest fir roots—
    the fungi seek you out
    to knit, parlay & thrive.
Humble-seeming pilgrims. Penetrants.
    Nets & nests of filaments, brews of cells.
We praise your frothy heads of mead
    & bow before your humped-up
fruiting-swells of fog & forest soil—
    your original
        time-lapse
            mushroom
                clouds.

Miracles

Alert Bay and Port Hardy, British Coulmbia. We take rooms at the
Providence Place Inn on Vancouver Island. The name is apparently
intentional as the motel is administered and staffed entirely by
evangelicals. This week they are hosting a traveling revival in the
conference room. We are told the preacher is focusing on dental work.

Yesterday at potlatch, elders
greeted death in the mirrored eyes
& supernatural dignity of cannibal birds
that stalk the community hall—a transition
marked by offering, story, food, & song.

Today at Providence Place Inn, the Revival
heats to fervor. Pastor George's Dental Healing
Tour crests. The Raven approves. Yesterday
Marjorie's fillings turned instantly to gold.
Hope burns.

Back on the island of the 'Namgis Kwakwaka'wakw
the votes are in. A crumbling residential school
will come down, its stern walls demolished.
Fade the awkward uniforms, alien gardens, clumsy
songs of false allegiance.

As the Kwakwaka'wakw say:
  "Afterwards, tears go away,
& yes, everything changes."

An Abbreviated Litany of Haida Spirit Beings
on reading Ghandl, Skaay, Swanton, and Bringhurst

First, we acknowledge the Raven, known also as Honored-Standing-Traveler; grandchild of the gull-white Voice Handler. Better not to speak his names, better to simply say • *the one of whom we speak* • or • *it's the one it usually is* • or • *Voice-Handler's Heir* •. No offerings for him, he steals enough already.

Then Riches-Tinkle-Round-Her-Ankles, sister of the Raven; and *Jilaquns*, inconstant wife of the Raven: mother of Quartz Ribs and all Eagle families including the Witch people.

The Snag who takes down canoes. The voracious Sea Wolf, *Wasco*. Sea Dweller, spirit of wealth, who can appear as a giant saltwater frog or, when dressed in potlatch finery, as The-One-Upon-Whom-Clouds-Rest. *Wealth has big eyes*, the people say, *and is wary of those he suspects*—so Sea Dweller's eyes can droop like tears.

The Southeast Wind, who lives beneath the sea with ten brothers. One is called He-Who-Takes-the-Tops-off-of-Trees, another He-Who-Rattles-the-Stones.

The spirit-beings who wear hats whose brims brim with roiling waves, and those who anchor the islands and quake them with their love-making. Whole clans of Sea-People and Forest-People also called The-People-of-the-Supernatural-Being-Upon-Whom-it-Thunders.

A diverse, lively, and potent collection of spirited ladies—Copper Woman, Mouse Woman, Dogfish Woman, Fair-Weather Woman. Ice Woman whose story reaches back to the great glaciations. Foam Woman of a hundred breasts spouting the sea spray of tsunamis, the one from whom all Raven families descend.

And of the Raven families—that most mysterious clan—the extinct Pitch-Town-People of the wild west coast. Of the last Pitch-Town man, they say, he was huge, barbarous, and could smell whales from miles off.

Honor especially Master-Canoe-Builder, well known as Master Carpenter. Beware Master Hopper whose body has one side only and is He-Who-Jumps-About-on-One-Leg and also that dandy, the seducer, known as Swimming-Hermit-Thrush.

You see, the world abounds with spirits and ancestors. It must seem crowded as a winter dance, crowded as a war canoe, crowded as the dreams of shamans who fast, except for that bitter-tang of that chaw-leaf, the single-flowered wintergreen.

Acknowledge all and at dawn, on waking, you too may greet She-Who-Makes-Waves-in-the-Daylight-by-Walking.

Praising the Fish

You are the visible whispering one.
The Brahmin. You are the flush of blood
behind a thin skin of mirrors. Your scales
are small as single notes. Rainbow above all

rainbows, you are jaw and composure.
At sunset your tail is broad. It propels
you up glistening into burning skies,
gills pulsing and nose to the wind as if

it were current. It is

the way wheat-land sunsets burn rivers.
In the flash behind flesh and the blush under
cutbanks, you are the rainbow of horizon,
thunderhead, creek braid and plunge pool.

You are frost turning the sun green.
And buoyed by an aspirated clarity—
all this air within water within air—
you are a towering splash of hunger,

our flourishing, transient shout.

Singularity

One bone achieves nothing.
—Paul Klee

$X = 1, 0$

The estranged.

The footprint impressed at noon
beneath a skinny equatorial tree.

A lone pick-up winding south of Medford;
its solitary headlight
| a moving gnomon |
vertically pierces the icy, temporal night.

The infertile egg.

A single hatch-mark.

The child gone at one.

One world, land, village, hut, chair,
hat, feather, rachis, barb and barbule
unraveling to a single threaded
dimension long as the coast of all Asia.

Loosed, no response derives
from the unmatched bone,
a particular nail, the last hawk,
Cyclops, god, kite, or necktie.

Six Haida Dances and One Application

based on notes from George Dawson's survey of the Haida Gwaii
Archipelago, 1878

1. *Ska-ga*
   The headman dances on occasions of joy
   wearing a Tshimsian cloak and a crown of sea-lion whiskers.
   The down of birds fills the air, covering the spectators.
2. *Ska-dul*
   is how
3. *Kwai-o-guns-o-lung*
   begins.
One, then many, dance in time to the tambourine-drum;
   well-dressed women are prominent, rattles freely used.
   The song praises dancers and house builders.
   When the house is finished, the owner's wife's brothers dance
4. *Ka-ta-ka-gun*
   with painted faces.
5. *Ska-rut*
   —a frenzy, danced for the price of ten blankets
   by a masked, mostly naked man who whistles
   strangely, then catches the nearest dog
   and tears it apart with his teeth and hands,
   proclaiming a potlatch of transition. A death, a tattoo,
   a new identity. Afterwards, the dog is appraised;
   the owner reimbursed. Finally, there is
6. *Hi-atl*
   a frequent dance of joy, often celebrating the arrival of guests.

Of the first encounter with Europeans, it is said that it was nearly
winter when a ship appeared under sail. Sailors in dark dress
seemed to be cormorants, which their unintelligible cries confirmed.
One would call out, all would go aloft. At another cry,
all would descend. This feat, we thought, seemed almost like flying.
We were much afraid, as was the chief. But out of duty he put
on his dancing clothes, and going out to sea in his canoe, he danced.

60

Semiotics

Signs permit no precise equivalencies.
Molds clone. Clones copy. Copies degrade.
Grades incline. Clines intergrade.

Addressing the small gods of the afternoon—
their short lyrical lives reduced by windshields
to sticky, barely differentiated liquids—we

acknowledge the importance of dark birds,

of burnt birds, of dust rubbed by wind,
the odor of ionizing air, of wind-forms
and dust devils, of lightning dancing out

of a split Biblical sky lighting the sage,
Lomatium, and the bird-sized shadows
that flit abrupt as quarks into the underbrush.

Saying Grace

Fidalgo,
the rain is too immense to ignore
and the fish eagle no longer sits high
watching, eye over one shoulder,
then the other, by the snag trunk, wind slashing
through dead branches. She is not perched on the cliff
rock, quartz-veined and threaded with metal.
For having lifted away just before
the slanted line of squall ran in,
and in lifting off clicked a talon on the rock
face, wings opening with the sound and color
of parchment and vellum dense with ink, pages
turning in a further room with the lamp burned down,
she flexed shoulder and long wrist, and squared her wings
to tread on rain.

Now she is the shadow behind the rain on a day
without shadows and the ominous flicker
the fish knows is not his, knows that this instant
is no reflected wreckage of his copper-scaled
and flexing back, but rather two further degrees
of darkness distorted and falling towards him
through a troubled surface dull with molten light.
And the blunt, intricate fish would sparkle
but for the lack of direct light. The opercula
flare; rakers, red gills, slick back stiffening
to a taut J.

The bird's eye fierce—the fish's clouding, uncanny.

Bodies

At the Haida Cultural Center - Skidegate, Haida Gwaii. In the covered courtyard, spectacular canoes rest; inside, rows of decorated paddles stand. The splayed and formal form-lines of animal eyes, claws, teeth, flicker feathers, and socket joints—patterns painted on both the canoes and the paddles: each living and painted joint, it is said, is inhabited by a tiny spirit.

Old-time Haida knew bodies:
split salmon and flensed whale,
harbor seal, otter, halibut, ligament
and bone. Each joint inhabited.
Old-time Haida revered feathers
flickering, prized dense martin pelts.
Still today, we call it curing.
Skins stretched, softened, wrapped
about us—we, the common surface
birds. Re-inhabiting. Trading.
Shifting. Testing other bodies,
other views and yarns. Testing
out
this variable world.

The Mind of Taxidermy

I.
What goes when birds fall limp?

The buoyancy of fishes goes,
and the subtlety of snakes.

What is preserved
by the arrangement of skins?

Some say nothing,
nothing but form is preserved
by death casts in fiberglass
hand-painted to the glistening
of living fish.

The encyclopedia puts it like this
"After death flesh decomposes."

II.
Becoming a Wigman
          after a story by Joseph Tano, the highlands of Papua New Guinea

Perhaps the young Huli warrior becomes a wigman. He weaves a splendid
wig from his own hair; then needing feathers, ties one thousand nooses
from the wire-like inner stem of coral fern—each loop the circumference
of a woman's wrist. In the forest he fixes the nooses to the branches of the
Schefflera bush and waits for the cock Raggiana Bird of Paradise. The warrior
has chosen his place well. The bird, not knowing the trick of nooses, catches
his head up to the neck and tries to pull away. Maybe the hunter takes only
the tail feathers, a fountain of salmon arcs, and frees the bird to grow his
feathers back. Maybe he breaks the bird's neck, skins him out, fills his body
with moss.

Finally, the wigman paints his face yellow like the bird.

III.
The trophy hunter, the shaken motorist
with a road-dead barn owl in his arms—
both come here:
     to the taxidermist,
     to the road-wise naturalist,
     to the hunter who was bone cold
          before skinning out the dead,
     to the shaman with hoof rattle, ginger,
          and blood-colored ochre.

Practicing in back rooms with daylight,
one in ten thousand has Leonardo's eye
and can make a chapel of the comely dead.

IV.
Remember the White Bear standing in an airport terminal?
Because his hairs are hollow and clear as good glass, he glows.

In Vienna, the formal parks are home to birds singing classical themes.
A special light gathers dust before falling through daylight on specimens
ordered, tattered, and ignored in the attics of imperious museums.

I have always picked up feathers and stones.

At fifty, my hair is finally long enough to plait with feathers.

V.
Modern cures begin surgically and cool.
     For bird or mammal:
the skin is flayed;
the carcass gauged;
the flesh removed;
the bones and ligaments
desiccated.
     For fish or reptile:
the body is sized with liquid silicon,

the cast dried and filled with fiberglass,
the blank painted sympathetically.

    Tools:
the micrometer,
the photograph,
the color wheel,
& notebooks filled
with a neat script.

VI.
Canny practitioners trade themselves in
for the best eyes they can.

Working in ash, chromic acid,
urine, and tincture of mercury—

they cure the capes of colorful birds;
pose their creatures carefully as questions

devised by the unusual scientists who
remain scrupulous to their curiosity.

They place bones in armatures;
sculpt them up with clay—

comparing always (as they go)
to memory, living and intact.

Then, with malleable wire,
black thread, the curved

needle green as malachite,
they make and hide neat sutures;

pulling each stitch up snug
and watertight.

Bursting

The sky sparks, branches light,
& growls—
    a tenor throat-clearing
that drops two clefs
    deep into double concussion.

Fist blows to the chest,
& a rain of great spare drops
    begins
whacking the leaves to gleam.

High up,
a solid paper
    nest of crowding
hornets hums & quivers,

while one of two
calm fawns shelters
    beneath the branches
of plums that split,

swollen with fructose,
    rain, &
restless ions.

The Hidden

for the now-abandoned villages of Haida Gwaii

Begin with our present, tenuous foothold
by the sea. Walk inland and the green moss of forest
will swallow and hide you. Paddle seaward and the sky will swallow
you in cloud and the village in alder smoke. The sea drags
our long lines down. Our halibut hooks. We have seen
the Strait swallow whales whole. Walk backwards,
this time time will swallow you whole, tuck you
out of sight behind the house-skin, beneath
the earth-skin, turn you blue beneath the tricks played
by light on water, by water doing its dance of waves crossing
waves, by the flickering of candlefish. Nearby,
you hear a heart you cannot see;
six kin-Ravens gossip over food behind
a damp sheet of mist; their voices like trip-hammers
striking at small, wooden boxes. Specific pollens are falling
on water, years hence they'll be keyed from layered sea muck
and bog varves: Cloud Berry and Calder's Lovage.
Stories await decoding. All these slights
of hand, smearing winter tallow
and the char of shelf fungus
on our faces to face
the sea with all its death,
all death's riffs and rifts. Survive this
and by the next turning you'll hale midsummer's
Fair-Weather Woman with sweet-meats of blue mussel
roasting open by the house-fire. Even ghosts linger
when they catch, as they must, the scent
of this rich and wistful world.

Songs from Wolves
after a monoprint by Galen Garwood

At the very center is nothing at all. Perhaps this is what keeps wind circling. Before the center is a blue singer dancing—magnesium burning with a hiss, a whistle he chooses not to hear.

Otherwise, silence.

Below this, an apparition—a man with the singer in his belly—appearing in a color lying between that of the moon low in the corn, of sulfur, and that of the blue gone to bone, a moon high above snow.

Beyond, all sky is indigo. Here there are wolves. The oldest chooses only to listen, stooped. She carries a forest of firewood on her back. Her hair is long, shredded—pale as Makah ghost masks with red lips crying O.

Apparition in the flame of the singer burning. Wolves in the flame of the moon-colored man.

Swells high as celebration, smoke, run in from China. Burned forests are pewter. They have given up on light—and run too, but like fingers, through a thirst of living things: hemlock trees, duff, and wolfhair lichen.

When the shadows from this ridge reach nearly up the next, the wolves, too, begin to run. Run down ridge-swells where kelp scrawls thicken the sea. They run through each other and sing; run through the world, breathing up the bodies of old elk.

Much goes into wolves: old elk, seal pups, shards of shade and bone, the mist lifting out of a cold valley, grass, blue islands, hair, saliva from their own mouths, even their own talk. Once or twice, when a man weakens, they knock him down, eat up his flight. Then there are the teeth marks on his bones.

But it all comes back, transfigured. The pointed tongue of stone licking from a wave trough, the piss sizzle at the verge of far territories, fir trees hackled up a backbone ridge, scat drying into elk fur, hair of ghosts, the song—

aa-ooooooooooooo
aa-ooooooooooooooooo
aaa--oooooooooooooooooooooo

The Lowly, Exalted

In the slow discovery of your home
how completely you feel your way.

Working among epiphytes and fallen
leaves—deliberate, silent as a separated
tongue—you push between liverworts,

nudge the double-winged samara
of maple seeds aside, and so go
further, slowly, on.

Maples loom and lean across
this gorge, this lighted slot of sky,
single October leaves dropping

a hundred feet in silent spirals.
Can you feel their shadows spin
and bump down in the dim ravine?

Our slight creek pours incessantly
from cobble bowl to stilling pool.

The thin sun ricochets and squirms,
lighting the dead fern—on the far bank—

silver. Hermaphrodite, glistening one,
keeled and skirted, slick and textured

as the skins of fallen fruit:
when confronted—your tentacles retreat
into your forehead,

when abandoned—you extend, languid,
deliberate; stretching for dim odors

and dusk—anticipating lichens, club mosses,
the mucus of another like yourself—detecting

as you go, in millimeter ripples,
every muted forest pulse.

Consider:

even the
crooked
pear limb
sends
plumb-true
suckers
skyward.

Boundary of the Worlds (*Xaayda Gwaay Yaay*)

At the fringe of this world, at the lip of the tide
raise your eyes from sea to starfish
from sea asparagus to black lichen—then
higher yet—into the forest woven with cloud.
On this thin blade, an intertidal wave-whetted gap,
the Raven strutted and flew alternately, coming at last
to the horizon where he squeezed his mind through, then
pulled himself after. Think drumhead, sea sheen, skin
of the world plucked, thumped, and flexed.
And there on a spit flecked with glint he found pale
cobble and pink granite, banded and conglomerate boulders,
and among these—one fist-sized stone white as his grandfather's
hair, smooth as if rubbed three months with the skin of a shark.
Also, another the size of a knuckle, brown as caribou hide
and set with nascent eye and ear, brow and beak.
Now the muscled land bulges upward from the uterine
fiord: forms of hamstring, kneecap, forehead, and blunt beak.
This is the Raven budding from a mountain—snow, moon,
and dawn all winking in his eye. The names for great stones
are literal: Fingernail Cliff, Talon Rock, Sleeping Lady Ridge.
Metaphors, we say, have bones. Bones that fault and heal.
What is more alive than soil, this skin. Or forest, this pelage?

The Mathematics of Hair

Long hair is the hardest of all to program. Ask Pixar.
And this we predicted: loose hair will not be deliberate,
as it is akin to the exhilaration of getting
broken-down cars to run—down-grade—by applying
symbols in paint and feeding them pure, riveted attention.

Rearranging Notes—The Montana Snow is Falling

Three dogs after ground squirrels tear at a ragged lawn.
Flints formed like four-legged animals. They are called *Iniskim*.

Willow marshes. Bear scat drying. Two circles of teepee
stones sunk in a century of hardening dust.

This hat-wrenching wind. This bunch grass flattened in waves.
These dried bodies of wrecked swallowtails lying in the ravine.

Breeding swifts tumble under the high bridge.
A pine siskin flies six giddy times 'round a fir tree.

Still we call the creek Hangman—after what our soldiers
did.

Snow blurs willows on the far shore. Goat trails, thread-
work fissures, avalanche chutes, neurons, and dragon shapes.

Peer through half a mile of falling snow—the counter-
current work of shifting air is now made visible.

Tomorrow may warm and melt-water explode ice dams
that lie beneath these steep fishbone slopes of snow.

Whose Belly is this river named for?

For Real

This trail seems entirely compelling—everything angling down into a ravine arrayed in three, pitch-perfect dimensions.

Take the creek-bend at the bottom: apparently authentic—dark water, graded gravel and cobble. Completely persuasive. I'm impressed.

And the acoustic enfolding—replete with gurgles, white noise, subtle echoes.

Even the flaws are flawless. This cedar trunk fibrous as bark—I'd say "seamless" but it's all seams, and that's what makes it so convincing.

Over there, a dead-ringer for a snag: charred, complexly rounded, six or more versions of moss applied with precise and careless grace.

Check out the impression of walking: variable tread textures, body sensations—each foot fall with a unique pitch, yaw, and roll; complicated tensions of the arch, calf, and knee.

To top it off, I'd swear the work's dynamic. Not just the creek water—that's fairly simple, probably a variable speed pump—but the palette of veritable details: the occasional falling leaf; the credible wren jarring the underbrush (or what passes, precisely, for underbrush—myriads of seemingly chaotic lines and moth-eaten details passing by in choreographed parallax). And not just the instantaneous and unexpected, but something like a deeper flux. Each day the entire array seems slightly shifted, a mite altered—evolved, even.

What would something like this run?

I want one.

Desert and Steppe Poems

○

"While your father lives, make all the friends you can.
While your horse lives, see all the lands you can."
—Mongolian proverb

Waking in the Desert

We are fed and temporary
events—

housed, birthed, and buried
in slow-melting & slow-gelling

flesh. We are verbs only,
moving air, dirges

and dances. Sight-lines, sung
tones all in a-blur, a-tapping.

Inaudible whistles, we are tugged
and shivered by mitochondria,

till out of the corner of an ear,
an eye, an owl.

Return

Near Horsethief Lake, north shore of the Columbia River.
From here She-Who-Watches *watches.*

Night and dry winds hurry at my back.

Eastward, stars and constellations of stars,
wing lights pulsing on distant jets,
basalt mesas, midges.

Faint yellow beetles and the leaves
of poplar fall through the wind.

The gas lantern hisses and glows.

Empty page, empty fork.
Can empty of beer. Broken seed pod.
Empty wind. Graveyard and plastic rose.

Empty shoe,
watch. Empty river. Empty
hand. Empty stars, sock,
sleeve and head. Empty

hat

    tumbling west.

The Salish Prairies

Before us, lowland forests

ended only at the water

or opened out to clearings

where loose soil could not hold

its rain. Fire swept the openings

clear, licked the dry and jointed

grasses up, burned the seedling fir.

Deep camas bulbs survived

to sprout, bloom blue, then go,

puckering in late May to seed.

The bunched grass called *Festuca*

(Latin for straw, a mere nothing)

still arrays itself in knots,

provides its browse and seeds—

first to feed the voles,

then through these—

hawks' eyes

and coyote's sure, light lope.

To the One We Cannot See,
Whose Name We Must Not Speak

Facing playa and bleak stones, we hear
no singer but the she-hoodlum wind
set loose to shape and please herself.

Tanked on a dying sun and rimrock-nightfall,
she hisses and whirls—her porous hugs
and hip bumps sap us and kill

each struck match but the last. She leaps
decades, lurches cross sagelands to parch
and batter camps and ranches with winters

too bleak and nights too black. Later,
a ghost wrapped deep into her cups,
she stumbles into camp without a cane,

tripping over pitched tents, slip-knotted stays,
stakes, stacked juniper spolt and sage stems,
to sit down hard on our little fire

in its iron half-barrel, flattening its guttering
flames to spark. A rude guffaw lacking consonants.
While beyond this speck of night-fire and whiskey

neat, thickened clouds eat up
                              the very universe.

The Rains of Darfur

I begin with no TV, no map, no history,
no trails, no kin, no blood, and no language
but these tiny 3-column-inch stories on page 6:
factions, horsemen, rapes, and bones.

So I begin with a 1911 encyclopedia:
"The climate is healthy except after the rains . . . "

"[C]hief trees are the acacias whence gum
is obtained, and baobab . . . the sycamore
and in the southwest, dense forests.
Cotton and tobacco . . . wheat, *durra, dukhn*

. . . sesame, cucumbers, water-melons, and onions.
Camels and cattle are numerous while the ostrich
is bred by various Arab tribes, its feathers forming
a valuable article of trade."

"The slave trade has ceased; [this was 1911] now
feathers, gum and ivory constitute the chief exports."

But ostrich plumes fetch little in 2007. The rains go slack.
Vegetation-stripped-village-and-water-hole-perimeters
eat holes where the desert grows; the hashab gum trees die;

and the sand itself moves—a desert walking south
at 5 kilometers a year. Herds waste and everyone
covets rain. Where it still falls on the terraced flanks
of Jebel Marra herders take the farms. Farmers kill

the starving herders who slay the desperate
farmers. In the worst years the heat lightning
crackles and an AK47, fully accessorized, goes
for $40 US. One for every man over 16.

In Arabic the dispossessed are called *Naziheen,*
and the jinni-demons on horseback, the *Janjaweed.*
In *Umm Higara, Silo, Kass, Tulus,* and *Ed al Fursan*
I imagine someone old chanting out melodic prayers

for that vanished and *unhealthy* rain.

Into the Desert

I.   Portland radio fades to road noise—
    the last news—John Cage is dead.

    Rising solid without snow—Mt. Hood—in an otherwise
    vacant sky, twisted rock heats up once again.

    Just past noon grey bark of yellow pines turns
    to old burnt iron, bordered & incised

    —black fissures, columns, pillars of lava, juniper.
    Beyond Crooked River Reservoir—3 pronghorn run.

    Most always, the high desert spare as drought;
    by dusk, jackrabbits. One careens from some pursuit,

    slams into the driver's side headlight—BANG!
    & the truck stares left into the rabbit brush

    with one wild, jittering eye.

    Below Hart Mountain lightening snakes at the corners.
    All eyes, mice leap (*Microdipodops*!). Jackrabbits juke

    to extreme shadows—dim filigree; there are only three
    points of light in Plush and several stars between the storms.

    I slide the canopy windows open; the wind shakes
    & blows a whole night of sage overhead.

II.   Chill morning, still now—eye of sun opening
    empty Hart Lake—full only of air drying.

    Walking from the long mountain's shadow
    into this lake of air; mussel shells glint—

empty wings half-embedded. Further along,
an old grove, rooted in hidden water: a great owl

hunches into day—high, quiet in cottonwood.
Riddling kingfisher rattles to no apparent fish.

The road is silt, snakes south, breaks trail
at the sharp shadow of the escarpment, walks—

in due time—through the place of fallen boulders,
place of glyphs and old drawings on stone.

Boulders, each backlit, hooded with the white
guano of a needle-billed bird that shimmers:

flight and glow mistaken for a moment of water.
Glyphed circle pairs, meanders, wild sheep, lizards.

Lizards that pass themselves in stone to sun
and quicken.

III. I have not learned the patience of stones.
     Vowels endless as drought; consonants fundamental,

        faults grating like glottal stops stuck
        in a crusted throat, thrust screeching

        quake by quake into ranges, broken.

        This stade warms and wanes, centuries blink;
        lakes are dust, salt, huge

        alkali clouds, fires without forests, blistering
        wind. With water goes a little arrogance, a little

        certainty. If I imagine old men, teeth brown,
        worn, only a hint of water in the land,

they squint into the sun & grin—do not speak—
sparing nothing, poor enough to sing, to draw

from, not to, themselves: these graphic gestures
that no longer bear water, these drawings on stone.

Moon from Winter Ridge
for Sam Hamill

The moon is a stone mirror.
We forget that.
Its reflection
from the valley
of polished water,
austere as stopped time,
is the double ricochet of sunlight
banking precisely home to each attentive eye.

Two Playa Sketches

I.
A pair
of red-shafted flickers work
    the spring-yellowed willows.

One
lands, tail feathers—flared vivid
    in the first morning light—

an arc
of burnt-orange glowing,
    a Chinese fan flicked open,
    braking against the flight-wind—

each
feather distinct as a pleat drawn
    to a nib, each precise

tint
of ochre, both raw and scorched,
    in defined resilience.

II.

The basin is a broad mortar. The winds are determined pestles.

In the turbulence of afternoon—dust blooms from the lake margins—

an alkali bright as salt. Mirrored clouds billowing white as cumulous.

Time, you see, is an alchemist in a cloak of dust and vapor.

She conjures a shroud animated, a land desiccated

and lifting in the silence of distance—in the distance

of silence,

in the birdsong at hand.

3 AM. Page Springs. Blitzen Drainage.

our tent glows, barely
a concise taut dome lit
by feeble head lamps.

a single frog chirp
tentative in the deepening
chill. the late moon, all

but hidden, must be rising
to the east behind rimrock.
obsidian above & between

so many sharp & brittle stars.

Broke

Eastern Oregon, between Silver Lake and Christmas
Valley—names that say a lot about how the Old World

saw and twisted the New—the few rough tracks
running south peter out at taut barbed-wire fences

and abandoned shacks. Wind buffets the sage
and horned larks persist one more spring, sending

their slender calls lisping from boulders. One short
run ends at a wrecked trailer. Windows busted out.

Door banging. Packrat nest. Two chewed-up kids'
books lie on the floor: one *What Happens at the Zoo,*

the other imitates voices of domesticated beasts.
Out back, clear tracks mark where a truck has backed

and pivoted to discard a coyote. Eyes intact. No flies.
It's cold. His carcass, back legs splayed, lies castrated.

Coda

Later, after a week of hard weather
—ice pellets and threshing winds—

two ravens and a magpie rise
from the now-jostled body.

His eyes have been eaten.
His fur ruffs in the gusting wind.

Baja Noir

We beach our kayaks on the sand-
stone *Punta Gata*, its articulated
cliffs burnt to the ferrous of coals

or crab shells. Sleek vultures perch
atop huge, white, whale vertebrae:
sperm remains, a backbone. Among

boulders, isopods work the shadows,
skitter like loose fingers till the full
moon, flattened as fire, rises

from the sea and this self-same
sea rolls back from freshly unmarked
sands. At dusk crepuscular

coyotes trot the beach; long-legged
green-crabs scramble from their womb
burrows to sketch plural excursions

beneath the broadcast, moon-struck
sea-birds who have altered all
the protocols of night to seize

lithe moon-lit minnows whole.
Behold, beached cuttlefish and hefty
squid ink the wave-lap.

Scorpions fluoresce in the stranded
wrack—a hidden
delicate lethality—

till, at dawn, an inland, dented pickup
creeps to market so full of oranges
its bed thuds, scrapes, and shoots

sparks. The west-setting moon has,
all up and down this harsh and fecund
coast, settled into empty cactus arms.

The Khongor Dunes of Honoryn Els

the dune insentient hums, with near-numberless grains so granitic billion,
    so unsettled
you can hear them in curved serration and minions sing. sand-storms blast
    and jig them
nascent from their home-stone cliffs and arid peaks. venturi winds between
    close valley

ranges repuzzle all that grit, that finite abrasion, those small saltations
    to morph
the wind-load into reclining dunes, nudes, blonde Mongolian braids with
    shadowed edges,
and long soft-crawling sculptures that tower now against a downward
    sliding sun.

sparse grasses sketch, each by each, a compass-full of mandala arcs
    sweeping through
the rough and loosely gathered crystals. bone will turn to sand, sand revert
    to songs,
tumbling dice—cast down, descending the longest slopes of smallest stairs
    continuously.

a wind is rubbing the near-dead heat against an upward pallid sky. the hiss,
    the wing. stalking
dunes are not tombs at all—for, far below, their drawn hems reveal springs
    where herds of camels
congregate to quench, graze, and rejuvenate their allegiances to these restive
    Gobi sands.

Bou Jeloud. Father of Skins.

Nothing I know quite quenches the once-necessary hungers:
the root after water, a face in the rain.
Can we be satisfied with this once-adequate paradise?

The goat has risen on his precisely crooked legs
and, more nimble than fire, has completely consumed
the last desert thornbush.

In his solo rough-tongued clamor he has now come down
from grazing the stones of Wyoming and Morocco
—The Atlases and The Winds—

to be retrieved, bucking and rank, by herdsmen;
sacrificed in the dark with stained and pitted knives;
skinned by memory.

Memory older than Abraham. Ishmael. Isaac.

Passing for Pan (that half-man) someone is sewn into the fresh,
    gland-scented, greasy pelt.
Is it this year's youth charged with dispensing the luck we have always
    called fertility?
With busking for the musicians of *Jajouka*?

Land of dust and goat fat. Musk and blood. Flute and dart.

Dancing, the goatman shakes—
his cloven hooves, his branch, his flour sack of pollen.
Pay him and you're potent, pregnant.
Stiff him and you're barren, broke.

Musicians draw out long whirling notes.
Flutes tempt the desert bones to tremble, tremble, drum, and rise.

First, out of the trance of instinct,
lovers must invent or find, practice and perfect, introductory dances that
evoke, at least,
simple acquiescence.

That odor? That is skin.

Bou Jeloud

A Profusion of Parallel Tracks: Why Mongolian Roads of Dirt and Gravel Branch, Multiply, and Fuse Endlessly

Whether crossing mountains, steppes,
or the Gobi, we meet no fences.

The way is paved with fragments
of bone; the insistent long lift
of winds that breathe out sage

& the fragrance of crushed onion sprigs.
We are our own police. And though there
are few bridges, we will find a thousand

fords. Having learned from nimble horses,
to innovate—we dodge the washboard rattle,
the boil of dust, the shock-shattering potholes,

& winter's brickhard ruts. We juke the herds
of random camels & randy goats that balk & bolt

to uncertain rhythms. We make do.

You dally, my friend, & I will swing wide
                      & forge another passing lane.

On Watching the Film: Khadak

The world is a very old man.
They have filled his ragged desert with lies.
A demonic Neil Young; helpless before his ecstasy.
The wind rides a Chinese pony; a great yellow eagle plummets.
After wolves, pavement. After gasoline, the earth.
You will climb a dune of killed fish. I will watch.
A tree, an icy wind, a slurry of bones.

Ovoo: The Sacred Cairn

In Mongolian: ᠣᠪᠣᠭ᠎ᠠ

In every high and holy place:
a horse of mist, a wind-struck tree.

A view that closes, a cloud that opens.
Dust before lightning, ravens before

the rapid shift of shadows, wolves.
When a shaman dies, the third soul stays.

Bundle up the bones. Peel the pine
bark deftly back. Carve a living

coffin clean. Bones will seal
in cambium. *Gazriin Ezen*, hear us.

Receive our stones, our coins, the smoke
of burning juniper, the hand's flickered

gesture strewing fermented mare's milk.
Five neat stacks of stone, poles, and prayer

flags, seven horse skulls in a row, some
crushed, some with *khadaks* of silk and sky

threaded through the sockets of their eyes.
A blink, and afterwards eight generations

of wind eating stone, light eating shadows.
The spirits might forget our names, but

vigilant as the moon guarding a mouse hole
they gobble up our gifts, scurry, sigh,

and when it matters most,
we ask that they reciprocate.

Spring in Wenatchee, Chelan, and Entiat

In this tactile land—hide, sage, and
native willows imbricate the draws.
Yellow, yellow, a meadowlark
rests between my thumbs and calls.

This early in the year, bare apple
trunks reach up from terraces—
hands twisted in neat, gray,
gnarled rows. Something that barely

beats against the skin is draped
on high-bone ridges. Now in the arid
morning light—blue and frigid—
a thin County man walks for miles,

making sure the trees pulled
down for taxes burn to ash
completely.

Home

The place where I was born—nearly seventy years ago—is
    called Spokane.
The American West. Pines and wildflowers among
    mountains to the north;
dust-blown wheat fields to the south. An elegant Asian weed
    called Crested
Wheatgrass. And westward, sage lands channeled by great
    glacial floods.
Horizons, virga, dervishes of wind, thunderheads, a splash of
    rain. Ravens,
golden eagles, and every spring the most ancient of all
    surviving birds,
the sandhill cranes, congregate—tall, congruent, and
    jangling—beneath an unobstructed sky.

And now—camping at the edge the Mongolian *Khangai*—
    we move between hills
the shape of rolling wind, their wooded eyebrows. In this
    echo of the Palouse,
its loess: grasshoppers startle and burst the sunlight as if
    shattering glass.
Demoiselle cranes hunt crickets and dance. Iron tools,
    discarded among bone
fragments, pit beneath decadal agony of hail and infrequent
    rain. One tattered,
imperious eagle perches on a worn corral railing waiting for
    marmots and Pallas
voles, then soars off in search of carcasses baking in the heat.
    I smell sage

and I realize that I am home.

Forest, Mountain, and Water Poems

○

"Another joy is finally sitting down to have coffee with a friend. The wild requires that we learn the terrain, nod to all the plants and animals and birds, ford the streams and cross the ridges, and tell a good story when we get back home."
—Gary Snyder from "Back Home," *The Practice of the Wild*

Entering the Forest

In the draws—bunch grass and antelope brush,
on the ridges—views to the far volcanoes.
Once the sun was on our shoulders,
                 but we have come west
out of a land of bone and leather, stone
and the harsh divination of dark and light.

When we reached the forests, low skies
with leaf-and-needle-deflected rain meticulously
shredded our shadows.
             Stepping into the folds
of malachite hemlock, nothing remained
of our families—wholly integrated into shade.

Horizons end here in the duff where roots begin.
Our bearings twist and seep, turning finally
into rivers, flexible veins of air
                      insinuating branches.
Give and recoil, alone, are required—for cedars,
free of volition, thrive without clever footwork.

Mist, haze, spores, and moist pollen-flecks bloom
and eddy in these groves: their near-motionless
interiors the seed of all cathedrals.
       Among the thickets and sober
columns unconsciously brushing our intentions
aside, even the wind sometimes drops to its knees.

Half the Forest is Night
for the creatures of old growth

Half the forest is night. Barely audible.
Yet for the adapted and adept, starlight
and skritches must suffice.

And listening near truffle-flesh, night-lives
hear the faint, faint gnawing of subterranean
voles, the squirrel that glides in,

scurries upward, then glides again. Each life
a risk. The owl's beak breaks into large, dark
minds. Squirrels' incisors break into

the thrush's equal eggs. Under the long
rains moss and lichens swell. Half
the forest is now water.

Warm-blooded lives retreat: bats tuck
beneath slabs of bark; gliders go back
to moss-packed nests.

The rain-full air sweeps between monumental
fir boles, not half so dark nor half so silent
as those nests of moss

where a dozen gliders warm their blood,
their huge eyes dark as interstellar space.
This half the forest is less ours,

even, than the day's. We barely know
its possibilities,

our own, our dreams.

Confronting Tenacious Forests on Steep Slopes, While Considering the Medicinal Yew (Taxus brevifolia)

HJ Andrews Experimental Forest, 4 October 2013, 3 AM

Attempting to speak
accurately
of forests

I bump up against
    —again and again—
the close and closed edges

of my mind—this cage
of attitudes that limits
the forest, by turns,

to *young and awkward,*
or *elegant with age.*

❧

Two friends meet cancer nightly
in the cradle of their hips.

These forests—beneficent.
Their tumors—malignant.

Each with no such intent

but relentless, yes,
in their endless bifurcation
and cellular

splitting—by daylight,
by starlight,
and in the shade of bellies.

Slough, Decay, and the Odor of Soil

log decomposition research site, Blue River Drainage, Oregon Cascades

Trunks, once poised and upright, collapse toward
a two-century graduation into beetle and vapor,
moss, conk, and seed bed—their boles intermittently
chiseled by woodpeckers uncoiling their barbed tongues
and probing the grub-etched galleries within. Hibernacula.
Loosened bark. Sap and heart wood riddled with crawlways
where ants stalk wood-mining fungi, where inexorable
ant-infesting mycelia reciprocate. The odor of must,
cedar disintegrating through pungency to pulp and soil.
The plush, ripe scent of continuous integration.
What seemed solid, stains and softens decade by decade,
to be torn apart by bears after ants—the flavor
on their tongues that of dull sparks. All is relentlessly
hollowed, grain by grain, cell by cell, into sponge and grub
dust, salamander refuge, slug haven, frog shelter, and moss
—all deepening to opulent, pre-ultimate, humus and duff.

Forest Breakfast
HJ Andrews Experimental Forest, 4 November 2013

It will be fall in a Douglas Fir forest.
Gather chanterelles.

Dry these on the counter overnight & brush
them clean of fir needles & forest soil.

Chop one clove of garlic, a bit of onion,
three large chanterelles. They cover the pan,
one quarter inch deep. They will shrink.

Sautee these—almost dry—just a dab
of butter to get the onion & garlic sizzling.

In a second pan, scramble 2 eggs, half
a tomato—diced, a splash of olive oil
& just enough almond milk.

Once the mushroom mixture has cooked down
golden, to the odor of a Sicilian kitchen with Mount
Etna at the window, add it to the scramble.

Sprinkle in a very little salt. Pepper to taste.
Cook in a well-cured cast iron skillet—stirring,
time to time, with a wooden spatula.

Toast lightly two pieces (hand-sliced)
of an intriguing bread. I have chosen an apricot,
walnut, & date sourdough from Mud Bay's
Blue Heron Bakery.

Completed, heap the scramble on the toast.
Eat it warm. Slowly, attentively
—thankful for the forest.

Encountering the Owl

... What I came to say was,
teach the children about the cycles.
The life cycles. All the other cycles.
That's what it's all about, and it's all forgot.
—Gary Snyder, "For/From Lew"

Resident bird—spotted yet hidden—silent and dappled
as the forest floor itself: that placenta, that rich compost,
that graveyard.

Begin anywhere. Ground-slope litter, say—needle duff,
the ground strewn with big wood, wind-thrown roots
and rot—equal parts earth, water, air, and the slow fire
of decay. Here fungal mycelia encase the threaded

rootlets of hemlocks and monumental firs—trading
sustenance from earth to tree, tree to tree, tree to truffle.
The earth's surface is, I think, a kind of skull for all the fungal
nerve-and-synapse-weft-and-webbed fruiting of truffle

scents that lure the red-backed and long-tailed voles,
the gliding squirrel, the spotted skunk to feast. All night
it's scurry, search, harvest, gnaw; spread the dust
of spores with whiskers, scat, furred and trailing tails
until the owl, its flight feathers muffled with fine serrations,

seizes the one less-wary or less-nimble meal of forest
flesh for night-long sustenance or the nest's fledgling.
All this soon enough returned—bones coughed-up
in pellets, vole scat, sprouting saprophytes, the blow-down
melting decade-by-decade into seedbeds that nurse

saplings silent as owls' feathers, mutually dappling
the forest floor: that placenta, that rich compost,
that graveyard.

Song to Wed By
for April and Tony

In one, we acclaim the craft of bent-wood frames, the rib cages
    of boats, cradles, and drums that carry us on sound and over
water. In the other, the framing of the keen, edgy exuberance and flex
    of adolescent minds: how owls cough up vole sculpture
and the bent-bone skulls of mice and shrews. In common and together
    we acclaim this ceremonial joining, with nodes, the nets of two
wide families—woods walkers, vintners, permaculture-and-percussionists,
    maker-builder-restorers, and open-hearted bookmobile drivers.

We celebrate this celebration.

This is a song of wood-benders and courting frogs,
    taut cords and class bells. A canticle set to the saw
stroke and the ratcheting racket of storm ponds, a *canzone*
    punctuated by the infant sleep, suck, wail, and squeal
that scores that ancient, accelerating arc of sprout and bloom:
    from attention to dance, from dance to deduction.
While the chorus—this congregation of biological musicians,
    in-laws, naturalists, magicians and scofflaws—pitches
in with salads, baked deserts, and the polyphonic caw & crow,
    yip & yowl, murmur & low overlapping talk of conspiratorial
celebrants: a fugue woven of cross-tribe affiliations, kin-traditions
    and a shy folk-wisdom that understands

that we see just a fraction of what is true.
This Sicilian saying, for one, might do:
Unu sulu nun è bonu mancu 'n paradisu.
"Even in Paradise, being alone is no good."

Here at the edge of this ancient hemlock-fir-salal-and-sword-fern forest,
    here in this valley of ice-melt, the clear-then-murky Nisqually,
here under the eye and loosening scree of the fire-hearted mountain
    named Tahoma who makes the weather and watches over us

dusk and dawn, we praise, exult and revel! Dance and sing and toss
modest home-made blessings arching over this new-firm-tied
knot in the family net—
blessings to April and Tony and sweet baby James.

November at Staircase

There is an hour between
the last day of fall
and the first snowfall
when the river is low
and whispers.

Clear as cold air
  the Skokomish surrounds
  old boulders. Refrains.
Upwells.

Sings softly old ballads
  of slow bottom rollers.

The Skokomish Running Low and Cold: Three Versions

No one knows what a river is.
Cobbles, in moments of god-like
calm, braid and twist the course,
the coursing, and single threads
move—faint cobalt—musing
as the rippled air.

～

No one knows what a river is.
Cobble, in seasons or moments
of god-like calm, braids and twists
the courses, the coursing threads
slightly unlike the shivering air.

～

No one knows what a river is.
About the cobble, that chilled calm
deity will braid its course, its courses,
its coursing; its many single threads
evolving in faint cobalt, barely
reminiscent of the shivering air.

Waiting Out Winter

Clear and cold as cats' eyes
Idaho nights wring all obscurity
from the skies: obsidian, ice-light,
half a moon.

Bear, he's had a belly-full
—gone cold and stuporous—
hears only his own dreams.
Smells sow, sweet apples, old meat.

Across the darked valley
dogs in barnyards curl smug,
secure—hounds that shout with half
their hearts. Coyotes, who maimed
them with escape, stop their songs—

listen stiff-legged for the heartbeats of mice.
A thumbnail deep from breastbone
to backbone, they huddle in tunnels
of hoarfrost—still, in the weak blue light.

Small meals at the edge of a galaxy.

Riddle Creek

canyon draws stream bathes trout dimples surface
mirrors canyon-above, trout-below.

canyon hides canyon hides dam-pool hides
canyon.

smoke hides canyon hides smoke.

fog hides smoke hides fog.

water hides water.

Perspective from Panama

An engineered bridge of water slices
through a tectonic bridge of stone.

Which, my friend, do you think will prevail?

Icicle Creek

Caddis flies walk the circle of lantern-light,
their antennae quivering.

Orion rises behind the Enchantments.

All night
a warm, down-valley wind
& the ratcheting pulse of crickets.

Storm over Palenque and Dream

Above the river called My Language,
male howlers grind and growl

entwined in canopy; the rising storm
engulfs them. She-monkeys bear

their young away, swinging silently
branch to branch. There is no jazz

like a jungle storm. No drummer with
as many wild and waling arms. Big rain,

the tossing sweep of forest, and afterwards,
jade feathers falling visibly from quetzals.

Priests and kings, each with an attendant
dwarf, once received huge snakes here

then feasted on the crocodile. Now all
lie buried in cinnabar where ceramic

whistles, the shape of aching widows,
weep. The Milky Way goes up in smoke.

Poem for Tokeland Eroding

The sea hisses at the lifted land;
erases, wave by wave, our footing
and the slap of a flat rain stiffens.

The bay is naming itself Willapa,
inhaling two fathom tides
over insubstantial sand.
Storm surf steepens the beach,
tears out trees, stretches
the grey beach north,
and sends two crab boats down.

The winter, the sea, they do what they want—
slam dance with the headland,
set steel roofs to hum and moan,
drop double-wides into the huge thump
as swells collapse; lick and slice
the westering highway off.

Sand, too transient for maps to name,
and seaward—shoalwater—not even ink,
but gaps in charts, accidentals,
the tug of a hidden moon swung hard
against horizons: bathymetry
ceaselessly shifted by great storms.

Yellowstone

Light is a hammer.
Ice, a knife.
The earth, a bubble
of hot stone.

Virga and geyser,
sulfur and lightning
—not hell—but
pulsing birth,

growth and collapse.
Drifts sculpt
the bison's great
neck, rivers

the otter's pulse
and undulation,
and winter's wolves
—the perseverance

of elk.

Ending the Kenai Summer

September, and mountainsides of bloomed-out
fireweed set their hesitant seeds adrift.

Masked for sex then death, crimson sockeye spar
and spawn till, played out, they roll—stunned—

drift and wash ashore on banks, shallows,
gravel bars where bears and blowflies wait

to turn flesh to their flesh. Magpies, glinting
of wet scree and crusted snow, prepare to go,

purling—from snag to snag—as sunlight cuts
the clouds to slats of light. The way is empty,

and valleys turn toward solitude:
           the wind and what it moves.

In Praise of Birds

O

Greek legend has it that several Greek letters were inspired by the shapes/ formations of flying cranes—most likely Lambda, Alpha, and Upsilon:

Λ, Α, Υ

The heron—

its beak
a spear,

its sixth vertebra—
    an extended atlatl

       kinking the neck-spring
to thrust and pierce.
   Quick, clean, true.

Merlin (Stillaguamish Flats)—Two Hunts

. . . and falcons fly like this . . .
One hand, held high, claps with a rapid,
stiff, staccato wingbeat.
—Bud Anderson

I.
High in the spring bare cottonwood
    a merlin watches—intently.
    Bobs her head—fixing the distance
    to her prey, then lifts
    her wings and drops away.
    She is dark, streaked,
    flies flat and fast
    into the shadows
    of dairy barns,
    machinery sheds.

    Pigeons explode
    into spring light,
    their wings clacking.
    A racket of blackbirds,
    way up in black poplars,
    stops
    into silence.

    She misses, circles away
    over flooded pasture-lands
    beating her wings like applause.

II. Just west of here a dike divides
    the pastures from the Sound,
    from the tide flats.
    The tide is high,
    the sun is low.
    A loose cloud—no—

a galaxy
of dunlin wheels,
eclipses—bird by bird—
the spackled sun,
the sun stuttering on water.

Near birds stream north,
the far birds south—
in a slow whirling,
spiral flight.

Merlin! High shadow.
Tightening in vertical tumult
the flock draws in and up
to a cumulus cloud of synchronous flashing.
We hear their thousand wings turn
at once from light to black—
their one mind conjured
by and conjuring the high,
lone hand.

She perceives, discerns,
clenches, stoops.

The flock boils and flattens out
against the flood tide, splits
in two, hisses like a sudden rain.

Avid as the Ice Melts

Seven thousand feet above
the Pacific Rim, the cold Sierra
sun rises on icy puddle-glaze

where two pair of woodpeckers,
white-feathered heads glinting,
dart from sun to shadow

attending to hidden
young to whom they bow
repeatedly through twin nest

holes. Only the black tips
of stiff tail-feathers protrude
as parents bob and poke

beetle larvae into youngsters'
gulps, then back out, black
eyes darting in alert skulls.

Four birds, in syncopation,
keep watch grub flight after
grub flight—bob, bow and

bob and back out to glance
and launch. Tireless
for hours—

surviving,
by the barely conscious joy
of certain apt and avid skills.

Magpie

Magpie wears tails
& eats leftovers—
daughter of crow
& owl of Albion
she dreams on black haw
in the shadow of the moon—
pale owl, fully eclipsed,
old crow at noon.
Magpie holds tight to carrion
before licking her black talons
clean with a shrewd tongue.
She has pulled her shattered
brother from the incision,
the black interstate:
she is both sides
of the Tao. She is hungry.
Logicians are her enemies.
She makes her own nonsense
from plentiful incongruities.

Over Mazatlán

Frigatebirds whirl in far thermals, drawn up
in ash-like plumes to soar above stark islands.
They spin too far from here to discern
pointed beaks or piratical, stark wings.

Fish cooks broil the moment.
Taxi drivers carry tourists to their shrines.
Each peso is a wafer. When the hat vendor
heads home, he walks all the way in wave wash.

At night, we dream—spiraling up in moonlight.
Currents boil at our bellies. Slight odors—
cayenne and shrimp—billow from café and shore.
These birds have shown us the air blooming

inside air and how each warm-blooded one
of us stews and flickers,
sending up their singular and defining scent.

While Sleeping at Otter Lake

a whisper
a note
her beak
her bare leg
her patience

the lake opens

she takes a frog
leaves two tracks, then
lifts large with faintest
light into the soundless fog.

Great-Billed Heron
Daintree River, Queensland, Australia

Dawn stretches
from a single color:
charcoal from balsam,
blue to the grace that draws
nineteen cervical vertebrae
in a liquid line.

Edges of wings that once
held back a longer sky
smooth crests of hills
and now in landing tuck
and fold the wind away.

She hides in the open.
Obvious. Evolved.
Waits like dignity,
disappears only to frogs,
fish. They see one leg
still and think rush
or reed:
nothing fearful.

Water whorls spin
slowly inside and out
behind the slight
obstruction of her leg.
Slack water, the canvas
of unsteady waver. Meander.
Swell. The slight wave curls,
small tongue. Fixed breath

then stab
stiletto and no splash.

A Huli Warrior-Farmer Tells of his Valley
Tari-New Guinea Highlands

Our faces are the faces of birds.

Since the Time of First Yams,
First Pigs, we have carved this valley up
with gardens. Now it is creased
like an old man's face.

What we take from birds
is not given to the valley
straight away.

Understand this—payback
is between *Huli* only.
Thirty pigs for a wife.
Blood for insult.

Man's house stands here;
woman's house, there.

Man tends to war; woman to pigs.

About the gardens we keep walls
higher than two men. These to hold
enemies out, pigs in.

For war—we carry the cassowary bone
and spear. Disappear between gardens.

Then we show, armed.

South—there—
is the mountain called *Ambua*.
It means yellow, this clay

across our faces. Dots
on our women's faces
are sweet potato mounds.

Ambua clay. It is beautiful
and keeps the sun from burning.

When we dance and fight
we make our faces yellow.
Fierce as the bird that shrieks in trees,
the one you call Paradise.

The Urban Mask

○

"Civilization is entropy in drag."
—Tom Jay bumper-sticker

The Roman Nose

filled with sweat & sweets,
acetone & printer's ink.
Roses crushed & mixed

with diesel, wolf milk, & human
whiff. On the street—a strange
complex of tourist, stale sewer,

jasmine, & cigarette smoke baked
with bread & pizza. That Roman nose
for blood, stiletto, fork, & bleak,

bald power. Yesterday, the dust
of dug soil: stone, brick, mold,
& mortar. House wine. Carriage

horses. Urine. Today, burnt clutch,
mammaries half-revealed by fashion,
perfumes, pasta, swarming *Polizia*,

& by the Vatican, the Tiber's
thick, sweet, dank seduction.

Michaelskirche, Vienna

At eleven the tombs are opened—
vaulted silent alleyways.
The loyal dead stay beneath
the sanctuary—a crowd
of coffins, leg bones neat
as cord wood.

They earn their keep.
Hand bones—commas heaped in corners,
ribs (as parentheses)
and backbones, each column
the articulated consonants
of hymns and morning vespers.

Vowels long gone, decayed to air.
Each ending with a sigh—an exhalation—
a small black dot, period.
The air gone out of another story.

Overhead the heels of women's shoes
click on sanctuary tiles:
rosary beads, abacus clacking,
markers on wires in old pool halls.

Fifteen schillings to the parish for the dead—
toll to breathe the air of tombs, fee to work
on the puzzles of devotion, tribute to read
in this library of bones. To divine
some other meaning than the holy church
intends.

Found at a Homeless Camp
on a Capitol Land Trust easement adjacent
to The Evergreen State College

Among the 43 contractor-bags-full of debris (weight exceeding one ton)—
materials from what were once a dwelling in a cedar tree and a 15-foot
diameter teepee bound together with insulation stripped from copper wire:

Loads of visqueen & a pink plush orangutan. A rosary, a hand-sized wooden
crucifix, several t-shirts displaying skulls and neon graphics, a Bible, and
book of odd science. Prescription meds and a debit card, a well-and-hand-
crafted wooden case for hand-rolls and a lighter. One empty gallon of Carlo
Rossi and a spent 2-liter bottle of Australian Yellowtail. Multiple malt liquor
cans. A bong with aged weed. One Grunge guitar effects box—which, as
it turns out, still functions. One empty can of watermelon-flavored Four
Loko (12% alcohol). A checkered pendant bearing a Maltese Cross and
a "Live to Ride, Ride to Live" logo. A mattress on which a long poem has
been inscribed with indelible marker. A small bag of coins from Hong Kong,
India, Italy, Great Britain, Spain, France, Canada, and Mexico; a token for a
bridge in Vancouver, British Columbia. Jewelry wire, beads, many skateboard
wheels & one wheel-less board. Waterlogged coats, heavy-duty rain pants,
a hand-drawn sign saying "Please Help", a small (signal?) mirror silvered on
both sides. Several cast-aluminum boat fittings, shoes, a cookbook from a
famous Atlanta restaurant. Condoms, unused. A wrecked Coleman lantern,
an Afro pic, a fluorescent orange dog chain. A soggy sleeping bag. A leather
belt. CDs featuring Jackson Browne, Steve Martin, & Lou Reed.

Deadhorse Flats
after Richard Hugo

No one will remember this flooded-out
town built on sucking mud, ringed now
by graveyards & Christmas farms
treed so thickly the ground dies black.
Cedar root-wads heaved up as windfalls
reveal hairbrushes tangled in the grass,
brown glass whiskey flasks, a bent washtub,
two blue translucent insulators. Waste.
Trickling between piles of debris a black-
water creek smells of sulfur where flowers
rot. Beyond the pale there is no still life—
only wire heads, a plaster heart, mud-splattered
rigs, Corvairs, a rusted road grader. Certainly
the blind man knows something of shade
& linoleum, & where Borax is dispensed
in men's rooms tactile as peeled garlic
or irony; an exit stenciled on despairing bone-
white ceramics. Yet overhead, the noonday
sun still turns a flying crow's beak silver.

Pelicans (Tiergarten Zoo)
Vienna, 1989

Old beat pelicans—
one with a whole wing gone;
sullied bachelors,
bills tattered as shopping bags.

When the wind comes up
they turn together,
beat what wings they have hard
and hop up, hop up,
agitated by some old hope.

South Seattle Rose. Thin Cat.

Unfurling intricacies—furies of green design—
these rose leaves rise nearly crackling
from fine-thorned branches dark as char
       & punctuated, like difficult
       sentences, with last year's
       hard, black, wrinkled hips.

Wild, feral, or domestic—
heeled in or shat out unkempt
       into this parking strip—
a ransacked snarl of rose
       leafs-out among
whiskey bottles, horse mint,
& flaring dandelions.

While beyond & half-concealed,
a thin cat with swollen nipples
slips into brick-lined shadows.

Bucoda
after Richard Hugo

The *Dead End* sign at 3rd and *Summer* lies
knocked flat. At 11:10, signal arms drop;
Amtrak blows through.
She's 10 cars long, southbound, and going 80.
The only road to town is blocked by one
electric whistle blast.

Three years ago, Sunday, the oak split.
Old man Meyers thought it was his head again.
The name doctors gave his wracking hurt
—tumor—made it certain. He'd been cracked
for years—tacking ferocious bills in splintered
windows: flags, snakes, leaking ink. "Prowlers—
thieves," he hissed, "will fry and fracture like weak
fuses." He knew ballistics and the law.

War put a plate inside his skull
that let cold in. Squalls gave him chills.
Before the roof caved he'd carved his name
in every dresser drawer; booby-trapped the doors,
chained pitchforks, saddles, Indian motorcycles
to the walls. Next door, Joe's barmaid said,
"When he died they sold his shit—not much
worth much—then boarded up his half the block."

Now every outside brick and window
is painted flesh. Kids chant his name in rhyme
and cross the street to shudder, sleepless,
in their rooms alone.

Brambles and Thorns—Ecopolitical Poems

◯

" . . . the order which the righteous seek, is never righteousness itself but is only order, the disorder of evil is in fact the thing itself."
—Cormac McCarthy, *The Crossing*

Letter to America—
A Version in Which a Mirror Shatters

Dear America,

Once you were everything to me. Sky and river; brick-cobbled and gravel streets. Brother and sisters. Mother who planted roses under your eaves; father who planted crabapples in your parking strips. Cousins, great-uncles— all roots in your soil.

You were the great basalt stones in the side lot, newspaper articles on moon-shots, and plans for fallout shelters with naive air filters. You were parks, pines, ponds, and the tough on 17th Avenue with a high-priced chemistry set and a 40" vertical jump—the fierce one who left you, too early, on an opiate high.

Through the grapevine, you were Motown harmonies in the high school stairwells, the mimeographed handouts conjugating German verbs, and the Goldwater in '64 bumper sticker reflexively arrayed across my bedroom door. You were Jack's pompadour and Jackie's leopard-skin pillbox hat.

Schoolmates died in you, America—one shot working a gas pump, one hitchhiking, one nailed by a speedboat.

America, you became a war. Again. And again.

I came to notice your age, your eroding banks, gasfield tremors, your young men old too soon slumped in alleyways like clear-cut slopes too soaked with rain. Your springs too full of trash, your falls gone dry and crackling, wildfires in your beetle-killed pines.

I've heard your aliases spoken in whispers and sneers: *Hangman* or *Latah*; *squawfish* or *northern pike minnow*. Some years hysterias swept you—witch trials, the surgical deaths of farm animals, rumors of abuse. Some years you were the distilled high-lonesome of bluegrass, others—the side-winding gravity of Chicago blues, and in certain dreamt seasons, the summers called *love* and *mayhem*, your acidic after-images swayed to the Dead by the Bay.

Your nightmares and memories still pulse with lost bison and salmon, with skin drums.

They are the silence we can't hear after the next-door pistol shot. Your Seminary Street tenement manager—he knew pop songs by the year and prison he'd been locked in, and looked after your cockroaches, your jazz, beat Cadillacs, and offers to work the numbing lines at the fruit cannery by the piers. Your fences peddled hot TVs and handguns. Your radio preachers stole from the poor and cursed the city; your cities shouted and moved in flashes and shadows. Your drinkers sang; your singers drank.

But America, you were my everything: metaphor and fact. Carnies and first aid, tourniquets and Kerouac, one wolf, the imperfect perspective from even your most perfect overlook, rural electricity, and reservoirs filling with red silt.

You were my hate and my love, sweet mistreatments and rage, reservoirs and bays recording the Anthropocene of western poisons and remedies in your layered silt. With elegantly engineered tramways, ICBMs, and your face imaged from the edge of space you were precedents and presidents, bunk and banks, courts and courting, the dunces and the dances.

Some glue kept you barely from rupture, until it didn't. We say *decay*, an imperfect metaphor. We say *fray* and *part*, *torque* and *splinter*, *blanch* and *fracture*. We say *disintegration*.

I who am you, beg you who am I—pull yourself, America, together.

Against Perpetual Fertility

Once, at small fires, we were cold—huddled
under the single blanket of the sky.

Now at seven (this year nearer to eight),
zero zero zero, zero zero zero, zero zero

zero of us, we pile up & witless pile on
the damp, transparent blankets of burned

coal & crude, sweating back to mounds of salt
under the clear, relentless lens of heaven.

Olive Trees and Karma

Pope Francis gives Trump a peace medal and encyclical on climate change, then expresses, with all sincerity, the hope that Trump become a tree:

"This is a medallion by a Roman artist: It is an olive tree, which is a symbol of peace," the pope says. He explains it has "two branches, and a division of war in the middle."

"We can use peace," Mr. Trump responds.

The pope looks into the president's eyes.

"It is with all hope that you may become an olive tree to make peace," the pope says.

—*The New York Times*, 24 May 2017

&

I'll admit to not knowing how this reincarnation thing
is supposed to work, but am partial to a karma
teaching lessons.

Say this:

Trump returns as a short, gnarly, domestic tree
bearing smallish, bitter, testicular fruits gathered
by Mediterranean migrants. A tree with fruits leached
in brine and lye—then pressed into an oil preferred
by vegetarians and health fanatics. May he stand
a century in the unremitting sun and increasing heat,
and have no choice but to be useful.

Clearing Holly near Eld Inlet
4 May 2018

Acres of forest
where a single
blue egg lies.

Elongated and barely
the size of my thumb,
it lies bleeding

yolk by a nested,
corroded Blue Rhino
propane canister.

A robin, a prickly
shrub, and this sign
of an upright ape.

Unintended Consequences
the Haida Gwaii Archipelago

That old story: *It seemed a good idea.*

With neither cougar nor wolf,
the deer will prosper here, fill
every locker with ready protein.

But the throngs soon obliterate all cedar
starts. The trees at the heart of Haida
being, die away. Even new spruce

are bonsaied. Deer graze the European
grasses that claim ancient village sites.
Without thickets, cover, or nest niches,

the songbirds flinch. Hawks and falcons
falter, while wildflowers withdraw
to cliffs, and the salal roots nowhere

but high on decaying totems.
Beavers, no longer sold for hats,
love wild crabapple into gnawed

oblivion. Seabird colonies—puffins,
gulls, murrelets, and guillemots?
Their eggs feed packs of rats.

That old story: *The fabric frays and shreds.*

Fish Line

A gull flies in all wrong,

flops on the jetty, head
laid on stone as if kneeling,
neck and head crooked
to foot and nearly doubled,

then lifts—contorted—off,
flies hunched and buoyant
into gusts, to drop, head down,
to froth, hard-hammered seas

and must drown it seems
but beats wings enough
to lift and breathe a bit,

then drops again—persistent
head pulled and bound
below the struck and heaving sea.

Mouth of the Columbia

Two hundred years have washed ten thousand to the sea:
   millennia of snow, bones of otters, mammoths, nets, bird arrows and
   feathers of birds. Ice-bound boulders larger than the grand hotels. Whole
   trade routes washed away. Skilled women gone, children dead. A few
   eyes left to carry the smattered genes of the Chinook—lost tribe, old
   photos, hand-written books. Tidal seeps, rain and slick water standing in
   the side channels. Eye sockets stacked in heaps, the white island—Mema-
   loose, the piles of skeletons, the eyes of birds, the fish, the salmon, the
   grandmothers, the restless ghosts of men—they carry stones called
   strength from place to place.

How little has filtered through these epidemics, thefts, the endless killings:
   a handful of painted rocks—The Spedis Owl, wild goats with back-curved
   horns, the counting marks, and She-Who-Watches the now-ponded river
   at Horsethief Park. Petroglyphs lying drowned behind the dam that
   drowned the Dalles, the spider-work of fish scaffolds, stones that weighed
   the old nets down. Spear points. Bones. Our short, uneasy sleep.

Everything goes pouring through the Gorge—cornucopia, mouth and throat of
the Columbia:
   fresh and smoked salmon, spawners, smolts, whitefish eggs, furs, hides,
   blankets, travelers, language, tuberculosis, knives, wives, dentalium shells,
   dollars, smallpox, words, horses, dogs, feathers from Mexico, September
   Monarchs swinging to the south, water, grey sand worn from the stone
   plateau, storms, months of rain, iron, seals, smelt, paddles with pointed
   blades, brown flood water, whitecaps, huge waves smashing at the bar,
   medals. The rum and oarlocks of English sailors. Coppers from the Haida.
   Beaver hats, smelly uniforms, potions, poisons, spells and powers. Stur-
   geons—20 feet long, 200 years old, a ton heavy—condors, buzzards, terns,
   and gulls.

Watching for Signs
Summer 2003

Some signs have the odor
of sand, rise up then settle back
    after floods. They are river stones.

In Baghdad, ragged children
glance down alleyways
where birds whistle like munitions.
Something going swiftly swivels to a fate
    bound by goat-thread and steel.
Mountains disappear
once their peaks are numbered.

The day unfurls—a leaf's veins
revealed. Intuition is of little help.
Logicians' ashes, forests' fires,
all possibilities ride,
like history, in thunderheads
    and wind.

Each emergent moment glitters
for the soldier—trajectories
of flame leap into his lap, curling there
like gaunt cats.

Some signs flicker in the rain and storm.
Others must be pried from the talons
of poisoned birds, implied from blues riffs,
or inhaled with singed rope.

Obvious signs are the hardest:
headlines, titles, the gravedigger's handshake.
These demand both doubt and respect.
This is why the blind excel in song,
why tremors reach the lame dog first.

Response

A poem for those who believe that we humans,
because of our special status as intelligent observers,
are gods who create reality—that is, the world—
through the beliefs and choices implicit in our observations.

I.
When taught language—the great apes first praise tickling.

II.
Given the possibilities, man invents the gas nozzle.
And as for worlds: Disney, the world of soaps, WorldCom,
Fashion World, and Madam Tussaud's Museum of Wax.

III.
Which of us has ever overcome the impulse to insist and prance?
Or to conflict and influence?
Or even to carbohydrates?

IV.
Maps and equations embed trifling gravity.

V.
Our purpose is, I think, innocuous:
to sweep the sidewalks, to enter
and exit bloodlines, to fertilize and fade.

This climate wrench. This self-built wave of extinction.

Once we knew the earth as: Placenta. Crucible. Mother. The opening hand of evolution.

Plain truths and entrancements—discovered, made apparent, then often yawned and blinked way, stunted, shunted, drowned and swallowed in the well of old memories, agonies, and adolescent pranks.

Our people walk now in giant shoes, well off the earth and insulated. Sit in plush recliners and flushable thrones. Perch at amplified lecterns. Helicopter in above the fuming lava fields—invincible in the blasé moment.

Numbing fear numbs attention, humility, gratitude—and the inevitable dissipation that follows, that leaves a restless incessancy intact is something hard to name.

[If I pay you to blind me, our mutual addictions are no riches. Right?]

What shall we name what we have come to expect? What we've learned to plug and play and plod and claw for?

Call it *bought-respect, apparent-comfort, amused-superiority, perfected-certainty.* Call it urge to still the feared-dead voice of stillness, to mask earth's whiff of compost, and the near or distant scent of *cadaverine* and *putrescine.* Call it *infomercial, sugar, radio zealot, acceleration, subwoofer, comfort food.* Or *Evergreen-shaped-Humvee-Air-Freshener.*

What shall we name each concocted wave of self-defeat and volatile petrocarbons?

And that other name, harder to dredge from memory or history—the rolling together of all names belonging to what we have lost or forgotten?

Scour up recollections of lost swamplands sucked into Louisiana sinkholes, sweeps of boreal forests stripped sterile, day-long duck flocks disappeared into lakes filled with bitumen sludge. Eroded coastlines.

159

Recall the Orangutan, Star Coral, and the Angel Shark? Komodo Island?

Recollect the herb that opens olfactories for the hunt; call up the map we sketch from memory in mud; welcome tilth and guano, the peregrine's stoop, the crash and tattoo of oceans' night-waves, the magpie perched on a mule deer's haunch, and that specific scrawl familiar peaks use to sign the far horizon.

What one name can we coin for all this? For all that's lost? For all that might be yet saved?

In(diminishingly)finite Series
the Peruvian Rain Forest

There are things
We live among 'and to see them
is to know ourselves'.
. . . an infinite series . . .
An unimaginable pantheon . . .
—George Oppen, "Of Being Numerous"

The imagination is always staggered by less than infinity and for our loves
we require perishable objects.
—Gus Blaisdell, "Finding a Way"

1. The Matsiguenka and the Uses of Plants

Yage, the drink of the Ayahuasca vine, speaks, teaching us:
    how to address the death bite of the *fer-de-lance*;
    how to forget by sipping the water held inside bamboo joints,
    which thorns serve best as fish hooks;
    that crushed, one leaf makes a violet dye, another soothes the bite of
    the bullet ant, and a third cures the ulcerating bites of sand-flies.
Place a sap-drop from the soap-box tree on a rotting tooth—the aching
    remnants will dissolve.
This mottled leaf, round as a belly with the dark button at its center, speaks
    directly: rub and heal the newborn's umbilical.
Spiked, but dark and oval as river cobbles, these fruit pods comb our black
    hair down.
A juice, dabbed on the nostrils of hunting dogs, magnifies the odors of
    rodents, turtles, and armadillos.
Small orange fruits bring us spider monkeys. Kapok seeds bring us birds.
Use cat's claw for colds, bark tea for strength, fig sap for parasites of the gut.
Strip the inner bark from the Cecropia tree—wash it, roll it on the thigh, scroll
    it out, knot it into string-bags—one pattern for men, another for women.
From these Obliging trees: nun-birds sing to the women; monkeys sing
    to the men;
and—singing back—we reciprocate.

2. North American Names for South American Birds

Horned Screamer, Limpkin, Plumbeous Kite, Hoatzin, Piping Guan, Boat-
billed Flycatcher, Yellow-headed Vulture, Blue-and-Yellow Macaw, Sun
Bittern, Rufus-sided Crake, Wattled Jacana, Orinoco Goose, Ocellated
Woodcreeper, Screaming Pia, Blue-headed Parrot, Cobalt-winged Parakeet,
Paradise Tanager, Fork-tailed Woodnymph, Chestnut-eared Aracari, Black-
tailed Trogon, Emerald Toucanet, Bare-necked Fruit Crow, Masked Tityra,
Spangled Cotinga, Orange-bellied Euphonia, Double-toothed Kite, Squirrel
Cuckoo, Crested Eagle, and Magpie Tanager.

3. Lepidoptera: The Scaly-Winged, The Many

Already vibrating, these morning butterflies.
Myriads of multitudes—
the radically patterned, the modestly dull,
the incandescent,
translucent, flaring, flickering, sun-loving
and crepuscular,
flock to puddle on shore-mud, cobbles, creek-sand,
and the tear ducts
of yellow-spotted, side-necked turtles
sunning
on shining river-bank logs.

Coal veins thread the daggerwings.
Star-marblings are strewn
on night fields, black 88s
within the swirls
of pale undersides.
Crimson, lime, and lemon
windows
in the shawls and shrouds,
the epaulettes and cloaks folding into brown,
shredding, bird-shat, and yellowing leaves.
Morphos—flying pieces of falling sky—
and striped *Marpesia*.

Metal-flaked metalmarks and crowds
of fluorescently-green-tailed day-flying
moths animate the tasty mud.

Owl-flap omens
(disembodied as two free hands)
pass at dusk,
as clearwings of light & broken
    darkening, disappear
(*escondido*)
beneath shady, riddled leaves.

4. Dusk at the Tapir Lick

An insistent, swelling din of frog
whoops, raucous macaws—
their screeches. Parrots—a racket,
a chattering squall, ear-painful whines.

Fifty doors creaking out-of-unison,
ratchet toys, cicada-shouts in tight
crescendo shaken like shattering maracas,
or a forest full of Japanese phones
ringing.

Sundown—this eclectic ruckus.

5. Diminishing

"The flashlight picked out a red eye floating on the water, pulling it toward
us as we in turn moved towards it. Manolo carefully handed me the lamp,
indicating that I was to keep it trained upon the eye. His silhouette knelt on
one knee and aimed the rifle. He motioned me to put my arm over his right
shoulder and direct the light along the barrel and onto the glowing eye . . .

Bang!! Splash!! White foam flew up . . . "
                    1955—A caiman hunt on the Madre de Dios River.

"Formerly . . . large caimans were so common in Yarina Cocha that at times the airplanes of the *linguisticos* had difficulty finding a clear path in which to land. The big animals are rare now—in part . . . because of the local industry . . . advocating their use as chicken feed."

1961—Anecdote from The Cloud Forest

In April the Peruvian government relented to pressure from unemployed loggers and announced its intention to let large mahogany concessions in river drainages adjacent to Manu National Park. A land rush of loggers ensued. Large-leaf mahogany timbers now lie stacked on the banks of the Madre de Dios River. Soon they will become $15,000 North American dining tables.

2002—Travel journal

"Mahogany is merely the wedge that opens the door to a whole cycle of deforestation: . . . only mahogany brings enough to pay for equipment, or a barge, or a private road. Once a road is built, less valuable wood—cedar, jatoba, and ipe—a rotproof hardwood used for suburban decks—becomes commercially viable . . . Charcoal makers burn what's left. The roads draw poor farmers . . . who plant yucca, scratching a living from the poor soil . . . "

2002—"Blood Wood"

6. Spider Lessons

The eyeshine of moths appears crimson and that of spiders, blue. With headlamps we find them in the double shadow of night and rainforest.

Nephila, a long-legged silk spider, knows moths and butterflies; knows that even when otherwise identical, the poisonous species will not struggle. By this, *Nephila* sorts its food, cutting the toxic meals free.

Mortality

O

"The imagination is always staggered by less than infinity and for our loves
we require perishable objects."
—Gus Blaisdell, "Finding a Way"

Rubrics from Northcraft Mountain

Working up-slope I have found a mushroom in the sun.
Each gill runs from the yellow circumference in—narrowing, closing,
    exact as thirty violin bows drawing together.

All this sun on brambles, slash, intricate tripwires, and blackberry canes.
Even the careful inevitably stumble here where the clearing grows back wild.
Thistles, spores, juncos—all sprout and clatter in the tangle.

Logging roads—overgrowing, red, still damp at noon, raw—cut
to the clearing's edge, knit there with trails meandering
from the borders where thin firs sway and toss down shadows.

Alder leaves fall rattling through sunlight. Deer tracks wander—stitches
across a ripped land. There!—the circus hawk arcs and crescendos,
loops trails over trails. She is listening for voles.

It is nothing to know the name of a tree or a stone, a man or a woman.
It is a mask without eyeholes or tongue.

Coming home, the down-slope chills. The mountain shines in declining
light. Streams run down from the center and out:
widening, ragged, generous

as an old man
           telling lies.

Everything Moves Down in Winter:

long mountains—wedge-like,
heavy as headaches
sloping into the fog.

Air turns to solid beads
and from nostril-steam
to ice.

Sinus caves and
honeycombs
of liquid
bone, even marrow
aches—the
lymph as

well. The eye
that's stuck
in place.

I take tincture
of summer root and

wait.

Climbing Towards Spray Park, Mt. Tahoma
for Jim

My friend is dying.

Today he may be fishing with his kids.
Yesterday he scorched the burgers.
My coordination, he'd said, isn't so good;
he'd fallen getting out of his canoe.

I climb toward the mountain's clarity,
its ice in torsion—the slow tumble
of gravity over andesite.

The fracture. The fracture. The fracture.

Up past pika hay, maggoty bear scat,
the last wisp of pine odor.

Raven flies by with a loud wing beat.

Then the two-noted whistle
of the Varied Thrush.

He is hidden in a copse
of dwarfed fir. His interval

is minor.
It always is.

For Robert Sund

in memoriam

I.
Shack walls must leak a little storm.
Breathe. Inside, candles
flick & waver.

Wind on snares—all night so
cliffs & shore cobble make
a Shi-Shi Beach
& silver boxcar sound.

II.
Where do we go

—characters, shack dwellers, dancers—

after the band folds
& all the books are shelved?

III.
Shaking off the night
rain, the living
are joined

by death—the dead
lie
elbow to elbow & low like the sea.

IV.
A skiff
your poems
     remain.

Finishing It
for JK

Smoke drifts down damp trunks of hemlock.
It rains all night. The thin soil thins a little more.
Nothing is rapid. Trees block and bend
the light. His pocket watch is losing days.

Good as dead, the doctors cannot save him.
The shaman cannot clear his throat.
Spurning hospice, he plays poker on the phone.
It's why he fishes—to feel the panic in his hands.

What Time Did

After eighty years
of prickly light,
thin as bent wire &
never comfortable
with cliffs: she
pulled the drapes,
fixed three dead-
bolts to the door
& wore her family
home as skin.

Passages

for Connie Behne (16 November 2007)

For three years now, you've written notes about that edge-dance with liver cancer: messages in a tone so even, one could imagine, simply, patches of rough weather.

And for wheat growers perched, as you are, in the wind's tough alley where soil thins at the hilltops and dust devils dance under shadows of an absent rain, maybe that's apt.

Today, the final message came.

These are my memories:

Tom spearing venison on sticks to roast at the woodstove—best meat I've ever tasted. Stories of hearing whales breathing all night as you tried to sleep on the cliffs of Galiano Island. Your tendency to sunburn. That early home near Hartline where you and Tom settled; the wind at your walls pressing and insistent.

Now I imagine, as in a dream, the last heirloom of farm folk: a mirror set carefully against a boulder, then the pickup pressing on, the road rutted. Days and seasons come and go. We have all seen our faces in that reluctantly abandoned mirror: clouds, bunchgrass, and a short interval of blowing rain.

Great Uncle Erwin

Ferry County, Washington State

Let cold leaves shuffle and fall.
September 1932 and a tree
kicks back killing Erwin
who's extended his labor as a favor

or as repayment. Near Hoodoo Canyon
quick death smashes his skull. Expectations
that had named his mine Cuba,
a dream of galena,
extinguished:

"a perfect vein" the local news
had claimed, "of silver and lead . . .

a four foot lead . . . that may widen
to eight . . . "

Heart Poem

Say *heart*: we think cartoon, ruby cutout, pluck.

But then it gets personal—the heart falters,
the troubled idling of a diesel before sleep.
On the track—bouts of breathlessness,
and in the silent ear—night birds' first
fluttering before they drop from the nest.

So—the appointments, cardiac Doppler imagery,
and the obsidian Aztec knife. Articles in illusive
argot. Diagrams, animations, wires, treadmills.

I've come to think, my friend, the heart is electrical
meat embedded in an arterial filigree. Its pulsing
embrace licks each and every cell—an attendant
feline, claws sheathed, and purring. A waveform
of ions, the whispering of persistent valves ushering
sustenance from the atrium to the tomb,

brush stroke and back-beat triggered by bioelectric
drummers only occasionally distracted by frayed wiring.

Linked by blood and tasked by flesh it beats and beats
and pauses.

Perhaps
to beat again.

Notes

Barbed Wire.   The fresno belongs to a class of earth-moving tools used prior to the advent of heavy machinery. Its name may derive from its use in levelling naturally mounded prairies near Fresno, California. This particular fresno was a two-handled shovel with a blade about three feet across. Attached by its chain harness, it was pulled behind a 1950s-era tractor.

The image makers is based on research into the creation of images (paintings and engravings) on the walls of Lascaux cave complex in Dordogne, France. These works date from about 17,000 years before present.

Myth, Wind, Stone, Seed.   A varve is a pair of thin layers of clay and silt of contrasting color and texture representing the deposit of a single year (summer and winter) in a lake or sea.

Two Dreams.   Charles Darwin, "The Descent of Man and Selection in Regard to Sex."

An Abbreviated Litany of Haida Spirit Beings.   Ghandl and Skaay were remarkable myth-telling poets of the Haida First Nation living on the archipelago of Haida Gwaii. Their works were recorded and transcribed in 1900 by the anthropologist/linguist John Swanton. Almost a century later the Canadian poet Robert Bringhurst produced deep, powerful versions of these works.

Singularity.   Gnomon: 1) A pillar or other object that serves to indicate time of day by casting its shadow upon a marked surface. 2) A tooth which indicates the age of a horse. 3) A rule, canon of belief or action. 4) The part of a parallelogram. 5) An odd number (so-called by Pythagoras). 6) Each of the successive subtrahends (after the first) in the process of finding the square root. 7) Something shaped like a carpenter's square.

Six Haida Dances and One Application.   The final stanza paraphrases Henry Albert Edenshaw's telling of the first encounter between the Haidas and

Europeans. It was told to George Dawson in 1878 and relates the native historical perspective of first contact with Juan Pérez's frigate, *Santiago*, in 1774. Pérez and his crew did not go ashore.

Saying Grace was inspired by the Morris Graves' painting "Fish Eagle," at the Seattle Art Museum.

Songs from Wolves. The image that served as a seed for this poem is a monoprint called "Anubis." It was created by the artist Galen Garwood and appears on the cover of Marvin Bell's *The Book of the Dead Man.*

The Lowly, Exalted. This poem was written after spending an hour with a banana slug (*Ariolimax columbianus*) in the Green Cove Creek Ravine near our home.

Boundary of The Worlds (Xaayda Gwaay Yaay). The ancestral name for the Haida Gwaii Archipelago was *Xaayda Gwaay Yaay*—meaning "boundary of worlds." At one time it was also known as The Queen Charlotte Islands.

Rearranging Notes—The Montana Snow is Falling. *Iniskim* (buffalo-calling-stones) are a central element of native North American Blackfoot ceremonial activity. Hangman: Once the name of a creek in eastern Washington State. Colonel George Wright killed the *Yakama* warrior *Qualchan* by hanging at this stream on September 25, 1858. The stream has since been renamed Latah Creek, a name that derives from a Nez Perce word meaning roughly "place to fish."

Return. She-Who-Watches—a pictograph/petroglyph located in Columbia Hills State Park on the north shore of the Columbia River. Its Native American name is *Tsagaglalal.*

Winter Solstice. An *amanita* is any mushroom of the genus *Amanita*—a group of toxic and psychoactive mushrooms that includes the coal-red *Amanita muscaria.*

The Salish Prairies. The (Coast) Salish is a group of Native people related by blood and language native to the Pacific Northwest Coast.

To the One We Cannot See, Whose Name We Must Not Speak.   Dedicated to the winds of the Oregon High Desert, as experienced while camping with Matthew Yake and Greg Darms at Mann Lake and Shirk Ranch. Spolt is a term for wood grown brittle through dryness and thus, easily split.

The Rains of Darfur.   *durra*: A variety of sorghum widely cultivated in dry regions of Africa for its grain. Also called Egyptian corn. *dukhn*: A kind of millet. *hashab gum tree*: A small thorny deciduous tree (*Senegalia senegal*) also known as the gum Arabic tree. *Jebel Marra*: An almost circular massif in the Darfur region of Sudan. *Umm Higara, Silo, Kass, Tulus*, and *Ed al Fursan*: towns and villages in Darfur.

Into the Desert.   John Cage was an American composer, music theorist, artist, and philosopher: a pioneer in indeterminacy in music, a technique in which some aspects of a musical work are left open to chance. *Microdipodops* is the genus name for the kangaroo mouse. The Dark Kangaroo Mouse (*Microdipodops megacephalus)* inhabits much of the basin-and-range country of southeastern Oregon. A stade is one advance and retreat of the continental glaciers.

Baja Noir.   *Punta Gata*: Cat Point, a red rock point extending into the central Sea of Cortez from Baja California.

The Khongor Dunes of Honoryn Els.   These dunes, in southern Mongolia, are known as the "Singing Sands." The exact mechanism of their singing is unresolved.

Bou Jeloud. Father of Skins.   *Bou Jeloud*: A Pan-like figure, half goat half man. In Joujouka, Morocco, *Bou Jeloud* gives the gift of flute music and bestows fertility on the village every spring when he dances.

Ovoo: The Sacred Cairn.   *Gazriin ezen*: In Mongolia, the master spirits of places—including mountains, waters, rocks, and trees. *Khadak*: The traditional Mongolian scarf of sacred blue—symbolic of the sky.

Home.   *Khangai*: A range of mountains in central Mongolia; also, the term used to describe the entire lush forest-steppe area north of the Gobi.

Confronting Tenacious Forests on Steep Slopes.   The Pacific Yew (*Taxus brevifolia*) yields taxanes (paclitaxel and docetaxel) which are effective in dealing with ovarian and breast cancer.

Slough, Decay, and the Odor of Soil.   This research site is located at the HJ Andrews Experimental Forest.

Encountering the Owl.   Mycelia are the masses of fungal filaments (hyphae) that fruit as mushrooms. Mycorrhizal mycelia connect fungi and tree roots in a symbiotic relationship in which nutrients are exchanged. Saprophytes are organisms, including many fungi, which get their energy from dead and decaying organic matter.

Song to Wed By.   *Canzone*: Literally "song" in Italian; more specifically an Italian song or ballad. Cognate with English "to chant." *Tahoma*: The Salishan name for Mt. Rainier. Said to mean "snow-covered mountain."

November at Staircase.   The Skokomish is a river draining the southeastern Olympic Mountains of Washington State. Its name comes from the native Twana language and means "people of the river."

Storm over Palenque and Dream.   Palenque was a Mayan city-state in southern Mexico flourishing in the 7th century. Today it is the associated ruins and archaeological sites.

Poem for Tokeland Eroding.   Tokeland, at the north entrance of Willapa Bay (the Washington coast), is said to be the most rapidly eroding headland on North America's Pacific Coast. The settlement here is named for Chief Toke, expert canoe navigator and leader of the Shoalwater tribe in the mid-1800s.

The heron——.   An atlatl is an ancient, elegant and complex tool made of wood, bone, or antler and used as a lever to increase the force propelling a spear or hunting dart.

A Huli Warrior-Farmer Tells of his Valley.   The Huli are an indigenous people who have lived for thousands of years in the highlands of Papua New Guinea. Tari is a settlement at the center of their territory.

The Roman Nose. The *Polizia di Stato* (State Police) are the civil national police of Italy.

Pelicans (Tiergarten Zoo). Tiergarten (meaning "Animal Garden"), the Vienna Zoo, is located on the grounds of the Schönbrunn Palace. Founded as an imperial menagerie in 1752, it is the oldest continuously operating zoo in the world.

Bucoda. Originally named *Seatco* (a native name meaning "ghost" or "devil"), this small town in southern Thurston County, Washington, was once home to the territorial prison.

Unintended Consequences. Formerly called the Queen Charlotte Islands, Haida Gwaii Archipelago—off the coast of British Columbia—is the home territory of the Haida, a Canadian First Nation.

Mouth of the Columbia. The Spedis Owl is a stylized owl design first noted in rock paintings near the mouth of Spedis Creek. Spedis in the site of an old fishing village not far from the John Day Dam and is named for Bill Spedis, patriarch and descendant of the Wishram chief. Another painted figure found along the Columbia River is She-Who-Watches (also known as *Tsagaglalal*)—a mask-like design with huge eyes and a perhaps grotesque grin. James Keyser (*Indian Rock Art of the Columbia Plateau*, 1992) says of *Tsagaglalal*: "apparently a powerful guardian spirit used as part of a death cult ritual in the early historic period." *Memaloose* is an island in the Columbia, its name derived from "Memaloose Ilahee"—Chinook jargon for "land of the dead." *Dentalium* (or tusk) shells were widely used in art and trade by Native North Americans.

In(diminishingly)finite Series. 1955—A Caiman hunt: Tobias Schneebaum, *Keep the River on the Right*; 1961—Anecdote: Peter Matthiessen, *The Cloud Forest*; 2002—the author's travel journal: the author, Travel journal; 2002— Blood Wood: "Blood Wood," Patrick Symmes, *Outside Magazine*.

Robert Sund. Robert Sund—the well-beloved Washington State poet, artist, Buddhist, and autoharp player—died on September 29, 2001. I never met him. But, because of his poems and the hundreds of friends who gathered in Anacortes to celebrate his life, he seemed nearly a friend.

Great Uncle Erwin.   Galena is a natural mineral form of lead sulfide—a major ore of lead and an incidental, but important, source of silver.

Acknowledgements

I thank the editors of the following publications in which the new poems, now often in revised form, first appeared.

2018 Playa Anthology: Two Playa Sketches, Moon from Winter Ridge; *Camas —Nature of the West*: The heron; *Cascadia Review*: Found at a Homeless Camp, The Skokomish Running Low and Cold: Three Versions, Song to Wed By; *Cutthroat, A Journal of the Arts*: An Abbreviated Litany of Spirit Beings, Boundary of the Worlds (Xhaaydla Gwaayaay), In(diminishingly)finite Series: *Forest Under Story: Creative Inquiry in an Old-Growth Forest*: Slough, Decay, and the Odor of Soil; *Landscapes: the Journal of the International Centre for Landscape and Language*: A Profusion of Parallel Tracks; *Olympia Intercity Transit*: The Salish Prairies; *Orion Magazine*: Struggling to Distinguish the Lupine Blue (*Icaricia lupini*) from the Acmon Blue (*Icaricia acmon*); *Solo Novo*: Miracles; *Terrain.org:* Half the Forest is Night, To Fungi and Their Hosts—the Intimates, Letter to America—A Version in Which a Mirror Shatters, Conversation Among Old Folks; *The Literary Bohemian*: Baja Noir, Bat Island; *The Sextant Review*: Bursting, To the One We Cannot See, Whose Name We Must Not Speak; *Turtle Island Quarterly*: The Hidden; *Washington 129 Anthology*: Great Uncle Erwin; *Windfall*: Forest Breakfast.

The following poems are published in this collection for the first time. In order of appearance.

Way-Finding by Moonlight, Tending Trail, 26 June 2018, Aphorisms, Minimalist Autobiography, Island Bay, Spring, Running into the Sun, Etymology of the Word *Solve:* To Set Loose, Three Interactions, Beyond the Copse of Ash and Oak, Remembering that John Muir Climbed Tall Trees in Storms, Granddaughter One, Talk, Assassin and Warblers, The January Floathouses of John Day Slough, Feeding Frenzy, Myth Wind Stone Seed, Two Dreams, what buds from the ground of being, from the root of life, Singularity, Six Haida Dances and One Application, Semiotics, At the Haida Cultural Center—Skidegate, Haida Gwaii (Bodies), Consider, The Mathematics of Hair, Rearranging Notes—The Montana Snow is Falling, Waking in the Desert, 3 AM. Page Springs, Broke, The Khongor Dunes of

Honoryn Els, Bou Jeloud—Father of Skins, On Watching the Film: Khadak, Ovoo: The Sacred Cairn, Home, Encountering the Owl, Yellowstone, The Roman Nose, South Seattle Rose—Thin Cat, Against Perpetual Fertility, Olive Trees and Karma, Clearing Holly near Eld Inlet, Unintended Consequences, This climate wrench—This self-built wave of extinction, What Time Did, Passages, Walking to the Edge, Heart Poem.

All other poems in this book were previously published in these collections:
This Old Riddle: Cormorants and Rain—Poems 1970–2003. 2004. Radiolarian
    Press. Astoria OR.
Unfurl, Kite, and Veer. 2010. Radiolarian Press. Astoria OR.

Poems selected from these collections were previously published in or read on: *Anthropology and Humanism, Appalachia, Alligator Juniper, Between Earth and Sky: Our Intimate Connections to Trees, convolvulus, Chronogram, Cutthroat, Fine Madness, ISLE, Krulwich Wonders—NPR, KUOW Presents, Longhouse, Moving Mountain, Open Spaces Quarterly, Poetry, Puerto del Sol, Raven Chronicles, Runes, Samsara Quarterly, The Pedestal, The Seattle Review, Under a Silver Sky—An Anthology of Pacific Northwest Poetry , Wild Earth, Wings, Wilderness Magazine*, and other magazines, books, websites, and anthologies.

Photo Credits
Flecks, Hints, and Intuitions: *Dosewallips River Valley in Fog. View from Big
    Hump*. Photo by author.
Cohorts: *Poets at Junk Castle near Pullman, Washington. 1970*. Photo from
    cover of *Measure*, a literary magazine. Howard McCord, editor. Howard
    McCord 4th from left, Floyce Alexander far right, author 2nd from right.
    Other names currently unknown (or lost to the mists of time?). Readers
    who can provide additional identities are asked to please send them to
    Empty Bowl Press (emptybowl1976@gmail.com).
Reverent and Irreverent Prayers: *Inscribed Rock at Ikh Gazriin Chuluu in the
    Mongolian Gobi*. Photo by author.
Desert and Steppe Poems: *Oregon High Desert Landscape. View west from the
    Alvord Desert*. Photo by author.
Bou Jeloud. Father of Skins. *Bou Jeloud. Armoud, Morroco*. Photo by Joseph
    Green.

Forest, Mountain, and River Poems: *Author on Sauk Mountain Trail. View east to peaks in North Cascades National Park.* Photo by Jeannette Barreca.

In Praise of Birds: *Snow Geese Flocking at Summer Lake. Central Oregon.* Photo by author.

The Urban Mask: *Naples at Night.* Anita Barreca overlooking west along Via Foria from Hotel Real Ortobotanico. Photo by author.

Bramble and Thorns: *Sun Piercing Brambles. San Juan Island, Washington State.* Photo by Ian Boyden.

Mortality: *Islands, Fog, and Bearskin Bay. Haida Gwaii Archipelago.* Photo by author.

About the Author

Long a resident of the Pacific Northwest, Bill Yake has made poems since the late 60s. There were years he worked lookouts, road construction, and cemeteries. He's fought forest fires and run a sub-three-hour marathon. During a 25-year career with Washington State's Department of Ecology as an environmental scientist and engineer, Bill diagnosed malfunctioning sewage treatment plants and tracked poisons in waters, fish, and soils. He teamed with environmental trainees in Tunisia and authored the Washington State Dioxin Source Assessment. Since retiring, Bill has traveled with his wife, Jeannette, to Papua New Guinea and Mongolia, to Sicily and the illustrated caves of France. Throughout, he has studied natural history, read abundantly, and thought hard about evolution and the place of humans in nature. All the while Bill has been making poems and images. *Waymaking by Moonlight* tracks these years and contains an estimable selection of Yake's creations. His previous collections of poetry include *This Old Riddle: Cormorants and Rain* and *Unfurl, Kite, and Veer*, from Radiolarian Press.

Colophon

Waymaking by Moonlight was composed in InDesign CC. The font used for text and display is Arno Pro, created by Robert Slimbach in what he calls a combination of the Aldine and Venetian styles of the Italian Renaissance, with italics inspired by the calligraphy and printing of Ludovico degli Arrighi. It is printed on Accent Opaque, an acid-free, elemental chlorine-free paper certified by the Forest Stewardship Council. The book was designed and typeset by Greg Darms, sheltering in place in the hills of western Massachusetts during the dry summer and deep red fall of the Covid-19 pandemic.

Empty Bowl Press
Anacortes, Washington